The cover photograph shows Ch. Galina of Colhugh owned and bred by Mrs. J. Gibbs.

THE BORZOI

FEW dogs can match the grace and elegance of the magnificent Borzoi. An ancient breed, his origin lies in the vast lands of Russia and beyond into other parts of Asia. There his early progenitors herded and guarded their immense flocks from marauding wolves and bears on the steppes and pastoral mountain slopes. In later centuries a more highly developed breed, immensely fast and with unique ability to switch direction in the hunt without sacrificing speed was used to course the wolf. This sport entails hunting by sight and the Borzoi, found peculiarly adept at it, was bred and kept in large numbers by the Czars and Russian land owning nobility, who used to stage great hunts which were nothing less than spectacular.

Also known as the Russian Wolfhound, a name which was adopted in the United States of America, its connections in Britain have been royal ones. The Victorian monarchy kept and loved the breed and by their sponsorship did much to promote by publicity its interests and development.

John Gordon, author of many dog books, has prepared an interesting and informative account of this prince among dogs covering not only his origin and history but dealing also with more practical problems such as breeding, training and general management.

Mrs. N. Sanderson's Sholwood Silvermere

Photo: Gibbs

'As I looked at her I thought I never saw anything more beautiful; she was a steppe dog . . . . her tail long and bushy; indeed, it was a princely animal.'

Louisa Atkinson (Australian authoress) 1834–72
describing a dog of Tartary, near Omsk.

A group from the Gazehound Family taken from Vero Shaw's illustrated *Book of the Dog*. (*Frontispiece*)

THE BORZOI

by

John F. Gordon

Arco Publishing Company, Inc.
New York

Published in 1974 by Arco Publishing Company, Inc.
219 Park Avenue South, New York, N.Y. 10003
Copyright © 1973 by John F. Gordon
All rights reserved
Library of Congress Catalog Card Number 73–91147

ISBN 0–668–03434–3

Printed in Great Britain

Contents

Preface

I⏢ has taken many centuries to produce to its present excellence the dog we know today as the Borzoi. That our modern fanciers' homes, kennels and show benches are graced by such beautiful and elegant hounds gives living proof to the successes achieved initially by Russian sportsmen who bred and used him for the essentially hard practical sport of coursing the wolf and later by enthusiasts in the Western Hemisphere and New World whose interests in him were perhaps more aesthetic.

The study of the Borzoi's history and part he played in the chase is a fascinating and absorbing research. Unfortunately, there remains little new for me to record, most of it having been chronicled before by worthier pens than mine. I have perforce covered his origin and history briefly, yet enough to show this magnificent hound's early and royal Russian background and emphasize his unique verve, dash, strength and stylishness.

The Borzoi fortunately, is not a breed which commercialism has touched upon with grabbing hands. Pray that it may never do so for when this happens, it sounds usually a breed's death knell.

I would like to thank not only the Kennel Club, always helpful to the earnest writer with facts and figures, but Mr. F. N. Chadwick of Billingshurst and Eileen Ruggles who among other leading lights in Borzois, have been so encouraging and assisting with fine photographs and advice.

Romford.   J.F.G.

List of Illustrations

Chapter 1

Origin and History

THE Borzoi's beginnings lie far back in the Dark Ages of Russia and the vast lands which adjoin her. No one can be specific as to the breed's origin in a continent itself clouded in the deepest mystery, at least until recent years. The Borzoi which bears certain similarities with such breeds as the Greyhound, Afghan Hound and Saluki, is a member of the vast concourse of coursing hounds which abounded in Asia and indeed today exist throughout the world. However, one is bound to regard the apparent feature likenesses of the Borzoi and these other breeds as coincidental rather than attempt to link them with a main tap-root.

All such breeds are noted for their great swiftness and have been used for centuries as coursers; it is because their function demands certain physical and psychological characteristics that it is easy to make the mistake of relating them by blood merely on the strength of one or two common denominators in their make-up.

We are aware that the Borzoi, more or less as we know the various types which contributed to the modern dog, existed in Russia, throughout Asia and in certain parts of Europe, for a very long time. He was used solely for work and sport, with the wolf as his main quarry. When feature differences were to be seen, these were concerned mainly in the matter of coat, some dogs being long-coated, others having much shorter, often rougher coats. Sometimes we learn, size would vary, although the big dog has always been preferred. The Borzoi's origin, although obscure, has given rise to many theories as to his 'manufacture'. One expert has given credit to the early Russian Boarhound as main progenitor of the breed. Another has suggested that the Borzoi is a breed developed from the huge family of herding and pastoral dogs, the Laiki (Spitz) which abound the eastern hemisphere. Russian literature intimates the likelihood of him having sprung from the old Tatra Sheepdog, an ancient breed of herders which work the slopes of the mountain range of the same name, being part of the Carpathians. Other breeds accredited with having contributed to the Borzoi's development include the Northern Lapphund and the Liptok, a mainly-white dog often of almost St. Bernard proportions and bearing sufficient likeness to what might be regarded as an early Borzoi to suggest some kinship with that breed. These were shepherds' dogs and the way they were used to discharge their nocturnal duties of protecting the flocks from wolves is described in J. G. Kohl's *Reisen in Sudrussland*:

'The Shepherds make their evening meal round a blazing fire, with their twenty watchful dogs encircling them. . . . They lie down for their night's rest in the following order: the old head-shepherd and his guests choose the wagon for their lodging, the other shepherds drive the sheep close together into a circle round the wagon, and form with the dogs a cordon round the flock. Each shepherd lays the fur and "swita" which, both summer and winter, form his mattress and coverlet, on the grass of the steppes, and all place themselves at equal distances from each other. Between every two shepherds three or four dogs are placed, also at equal distances from each other. In order to make the dogs stay on their respective posts, a piece of old cloak or sheepskin is laid on the spot. A mat of this description belonging especially to each dog, is kept for him in the wagon, and each knows his own, he is sure to lie down wherever he finds it. The wolves would scarcely dare to attack a fortress so well garrisoned.'

Very little information can be gleaned from early written Russian material, apart from meagre facts which arise from the records of hunting dogs which were used to course hares in the thirteenth century. Peter Michailowitsch Gubinin in his book, published Moscow 1890, gives some information as to the breed's development in the seventeenth and eighteenth centuries. The German translation reveals that at least seven coursing breeds existed in Russia at that time, one being wire-haired and others which were native to outflung areas such as Poland and the Crimea. He does however, mention the *Kurland* variety of coursing dog, describing it as ponderous and rather awkward in action, but huge and of great power. The variety's coat was said to be short, i.e. about two inches long and wavy and curled in parts. The colours mentioned are grey, lemon, marbled and brindled coats, the last being in different shades. This dog was used extensively for coursing the hare and the boar.

Many breed students believe that this form, coupled perhaps with the Liptok, already referred to, may well have been the main contributor to the Borzoi. The latter breed is likely to have provided some of the black markings sported by the modern Borzoi and the black-and-tan, black saddles and tricolours, disliked in certain quarters, may well have been heritages from the Crimean Gazelle Hound (Saluki), although this is by no means certain, at least from readily available data.

The really good type of Psovi Borzoi (a long-coated variety), such as we appreciate these days, had become reasonably well established by the nineteenth century, even before this era, and has been maintained thus as the ideal form since. Fortunately, it has not been a breed adulterated or spoiled by faddist features —it is still used in its native land for heavy coursing, at which it has excelled through the centuries. In Russia, coursing the wolf was a national sport, conducted on what was nothing less than a magnificent scale, by both the aristocracy and moneyed land-owners. Huge kennels were maintained and breeding was not only carefully calculated to produce the best and strongest dogs, but the methods employed were guarded with the utmost secrecy. Bloodlines were of absolute purity and the ideal type and temperament were perpetuated, courage in the strain being of prime importance both to owners and the huntsmen. Certain abilities in the particular strains were developed and became considered key factors typifying the respective kennels, to be preserved at all costs. However, with the coming of the second half of the last century, the old feudal system in Russia, already weakened, began to totter and many serfs, freed from their bondage dispersed from the estates. This did much to reduce the glorious activities of the hunt and many of the big and well-known wolf drives, because of the staff shortage had to be discontinued or at best run on less frequent occasions and with diminished magnificence. Nevertheless, some enthusiasts still managed to turn out their packs, at least until the Russian Revolution in 1917. Then estates were broken up and many possessions confiscated including dogs and kennels. Those which were not, usually disbanded their packs eventually, although a few diehards persisted with the traditional sport in a very modest way.

There is little doubt that the six decades leading up to the end of World War I were years fraught with some danger for the Borzoi. He stood the chance of extermination and might well have disappeared in his pure form had it not been for devotees of the breed who watched and guarded his welfare. A distinct menace to the Borzoi's purity in the latter part of that era was an attempt by certain factors to introduce the English Greyhound and Saluki and divers other coursing breeds into his blood-lines. Although this affected some of the southern dogs, it seemingly missed the ancient strains in the north of Russia. From these pure dogs, the old packs gradually built up again but with the paucity of Borzoi numbers it is not surprising that certain variations in type were noted, the same being true in respect of coat length and quality. Such problems occur with most breeds in their evolution, but soon become straightened out as breeding becomes calculated and more frequent, and this is what has happened with the Borzoi. However, the student should read (if he can obtain it) an article in the *Russian Hunting Journal*, entitled 'Borsaja', written by N. N. Tschelischtscheff in 1930. It deals with the Borzoi just prior to the waning period of its history, i.e. 1860, already referred to. All the types which existed, giving details of the strains by name and description will be found in this remarkable and valuable contribution by a man who must have had considerable experience, not to mention appreciation of his breed.

Sport in the Czar's day

The Borzoi's development to perfection was persisted with in the years which went before and beyond the turn of the last century and we are indebted to Rawdon B. Lee for his excellent *Modern Dogs* (Sporting Division), written about this time (1893) in which he comments on a description of the Borzoi written to the *Field* by a correspondent in 1887. The writer says this Russian hound 'is one of the noblest of all dogs, and in his own land he is considered the very noblest, and valued accordingly. Like all things noble that are genuine, he is rare; and, like many other highly bred creatures, the genuine Borzoi is, from in-breeding, becoming rarer every year. By crossing, however, with the Deerhound and other suitable breeds, the race will no doubt be kept alive with stained lineage. From the earliest times, the great families of Russia have bred the Borzoi jealously against each other for the purpose of wolf-hunting, but there are now few really good kennels of the breed. There are, I believe, various kinds of Borzoi—the smooth, the short-tailed, etc.—but by far the handsomest, and the only one of which I have personal knowledge, is the rough-haired, long-tailed strain. Of these, I have seen but very few good specimens in England, and, in fact, have seen prizes given at shows to very inferior specimens entered in the foreign class under this name. The true Borzoi is shaped like a Scotch Deerhound, but is the more powerful hound. In height, he should be from 26 inches to 32 inches with limbs showing great strength, combined with terrific speed power. Indeed, his speed is greater than that of an English Greyhound. This quality is clearly shown by the long drooping quarters, hocks well let down close to the ground, and arched loins of such power and breadth as to give the dog almost a hunched appearance. The coat is silky, with a splendid frill round the neck, well-feathered legs, and a tail beautifully fringed on the under side. The carriage of the tail is peculiar, as it is almost tucked between the hind legs, so straight down does it hang until at the end it curls slightly outwards with a graceful sweep; but this, like the bang tail of the thoroughbred race-horse, adds to the beauty of the quarters. The depth of these dogs through the heart is quite extraordinary, giving them, with their enormous strength of loin, a very powerful appearance, and it seems strange that they do not possess more staying powers than they are generally accredited with. The head is very beautiful, being nearly smooth, and with immense length and strength of jaws, armed with teeth which make one feel glad to meet the Borzoi as a friend, The eyes are bright and wild, and have the peculiarity of varying in colour with the colour of the dog. Thus, a white dog marked, with lemon eyes; a mouse-coloured, eyes of the same tinge, and so on.

'The favourite colour of all, and by far the rarest for these dogs, is pure white, but this is seldom met with. The usual colour is white, marked with fawn, lemon, red, or grey more or less mixed. Perhaps the prettiest features of all in the Borzoi are its ears, which are very small, fringed with delicate silky hair, and should be pricked with a half fall-over like a good collie's. In his movements he much resembles a wild animal, and has quite the slouching walk and long sling trot which is a characteristic of his born enemy, the wolf. Yet to see a Borzoi trot out with his long swinging action, and then just break into a canter, has always reminded me of a two-year-old cantering down to the post. The muscles on the quarters, thighs and arms should be well developed, as these dogs are intended, and in fact used, to course the wild wolf. Strong must be the muscles, long the teeth, and indomitable the pluck of the Borzoi, who has to counter single-handed the wild wolf in his own haunts. No doubt, the Borzoi, on such occasions, remembers the well-known fact that the favourite meat of the wolf is dog, and acts accordingly. It is usual, however, to employ two Borzoi to course a wolf, and it is only the best specimens what can be entrusted to account for one single handed.'

At this point it is of interest to note the method of coursing the wolf in Russia, also what the good Borzoi is expected to do. An experienced dog can often deal with the wolf single handed, the procedure being for the dog to run up from behind and alongside his quarry taking him by the neck just under the ear. Once this hold is taken it must not be relinquished or the wolf may well take the advantage. It is quite usual for two dogs to be employed when they work in unison, one either side of the wolf taking him behind each ear simultaneously. The huntsman is then able to despatch the animal with his knife or if capture is intended, to muzzle it. This is achieved by various means, one method being to get the wolf to seize a rod or stick (which he will often do automatically). At either end of the rod will be tied a thong and the two ends will then be secured round the wolf's neck, whereupon he will be caged and returned to the Borzoi kennels to be used later for training young dogs. It is interesting to record that in spite of the wildness involved in this sport, both dogs and huntsmen (*chasseurs*) frequently ended the day completely unscathed!

The Borzoi kennels in the early days in Russia were what might be termed today—'fabulous' and indeed they housed large and expensive collections of Borzoi. Lee reports on Mr. F. C. Lowe's comments following a visit to Russia in 1889 where he stayed at the home of a Mr. Kalmoutzky, in the southern part of that country. This gentleman being a well-known sportsman had just inherited extensive land property, and Lowe says: 'He has built kennels which I should say are not surpassed in any country—being very large in size, and as near to perfection in detail as can well be imagined. The lodging houses, numbering three, are benched on two sides, and at each end there is a room for a man; three kennelmen being allowed for each kennel, two of them on duty night and day. This gives nine kennelmen to the kennels and, with five other officials, the number of men employed on it are fourteen. It is necessary to have men in attendance at all times, as the wolfhounds are very quarrelsome, and terrible fighters. Each kennel has a large yard of more than three-quarters of an acre. In addition to the above, there are commodious kennels for puppies (and these buildings are heated with hot air), cooking houses, and a hospital. There is telephone communication from all the kennels to Mr. Kalmoutzky's house and he expects everything to be in readiness for a hunt in ten minutes from the time he sends his orders. In the kennels above described can be seen perhaps the finest pack of wolfhounds in the world, numbering twenty-two couples. They form a magnificent collection, their owner having spared no expense in getting the best to be found in Russia, and of the oldest blood. Some of them have cost £300 each; and the estimated worth of the pack is considerably over £5000.

'A perfect wolfhound must run up to a wolf, collar him by the neck just under the ear, and, with the two animals rolling over, the hound must never lose his hold, or the wolf would turn round and snap him through the leg. Three of these hounds hold the biggest wolf powerless; so that the men can dismount from their horses and muzzle the wolf to take him alive. The biggest Scotch Deerhounds have been tried, but found wanting;

they will not hold long enough. And to show how tenacious is the grip of the Russian hounds, they are sometimes suffocated by the very effort of holding. Some of them stand 32 inches at the shoulder, are enormously deep through the girth, and their length and power of jaw are something remarkable. They have a roach back, very long muscular quarters, and capital legs and feet. In coat, they are very profuse, of a soft, silky texture, but somewhat open.

'I took the journey to Russia with eleven couples of Fox-hounds, as additions to Mr. Kalmoutzky's pack. I had cases made to hold two hounds, so that I had eleven of these big packages, which went as my personal luggage, the weight being a ton and a quarter. It took me exactly seven days to get to my destination, from Dover *via* Paris, Vienna and Jassy; and I was met in right regal state, as there was a carriage and four for myself, another for Mr. Kalmoutzky's steward, and five wagons, each drawn by four horses, for the hounds, with seven *chasseurs* to take charge of them. We had nearly forty miles to drive; and the hardy little Russian horses did this at a hard gallop, over plains with no roads, and there were no changes. We were just under four hours doing this wild journey; and my good friend and host, who did not expect me to arrive so early, had gone out on a wolf-seeking expedition; but on his return, the first thing, after a most hearty welcome, was to inspect the kennel, with which I was, of course, greatly delighted. He would not show me the wolfhounds at this moment, as that inspection was reserved until after dinner, when they were all brought into his study, one by one, and their exploits separately recorded. Noble-looking fellows they are; and by their immense size and powerful frames, of much the same formation as our English Greyhound, they are admirably adapted to course big game. They look quiet, but the least movement excites them; and in leading them even through the hall, from the study, there was very nearly a battle royal or two. The Russian *chasseurs*, though, beat any men I have ever seen in handling a hound; and their influence, apparently all by kindness, is extraordinary. I noticed that even the puppies at play made for the same spot in trying to pull each other down—namely, by the side of the neck under the ear; and this mode of attack seems instinctively born in them. The wolf's running is perfectly straight, and if he attacks it is straight ahead; he will only turn if caught in a manner to do so; and a dog laying hold of him over the back or hind-quarters would be terribly punished. The clever wolfhound never gets hurt, no matter whether he or the wolf attacks first; and some singular trials of this sort have taken place.

'Recently, a very big wolf, that had been captured with much difficulty, was matched against any two hounds in Russia. The challenge was accepted, and the wolf placed in a huge box in an open space. The moment the trap was pulled the wolf stood and faced the spectators; on the hounds being slipped on him he attacked them; but they avoided his rush, and carried off without the least difficulty; whereupon an enormous price was paid for one of the hounds. The Russian style of hunting would not meet with all our English views on sport; but there is doubtless a deal of excitement about it. Mr. Kalmoutzky's domain is entirely on a plain, with scarcely any woodlands at all. It is all like a 'sea of grass', the going being as good as on Newmarket Heath, with here and there the land turned up in cultivation, but looking much like patches in the vast estate expanse; so also did the reed beds of 300 or 400 acres each, and these are the coverts for the wolves and foxes. These reed beds are mostly eight or nine miles apart, so English foxhunters could see what a gallop could be had there; better than Dartmoor or Exmoor, as the turf is perfect, no rough ground, and the hills little more than undulations.

'Special hunts would have been arranged on my behalf, but alas! like our own frozen-out sportsmen, I had to be disappointed, as frost and snow interfered. However, one morning I was given an insight into wolf-coursing, but one that had previously been captured being let loose on the snow. First, a very noted hound was slipped to show how one could perform single-handed. The start given to the wolf was about 200 yards, and in about 600 yards the hound had got up, and in the next instant had taken hold by the neck, and both seemed to turn head over heels in a mass. The next course two hounds were slipped, and these ran up to the wolf one on each side, catching him almost at the same moment; the foe was then powerless, and seemed to be as easily muzzled as a collie dog.

'I remarked to my host that I did not think the hounds seemed to go quite as fast as our Greyhounds, and he replied, "No, they do not. We have tried them, and the Greyhound is the faster; but none of your breeds have the hold of our Hounds."

'The plan of a regular hunt was fully described to me. It is decided to draw a reed bed, and very quietly a mounted *chasseur* with three wolfhounds is stationed on some vantage ground near. Other points are guarded in the same manner, and then the head huntsman rides into the covert with a pack of Foxhounds. The oldest wolves will break covert at almost the first cheer given to the hounds; but the younger ones want a lot of rattling. However, the keen eyes of the men and hounds soon detect wolves stealing away; the three hounds are then slipped, a gallop begins, and generally, in the course of a mile or less, the wolf is bowled over. The *chasseur* then dismounts, cleverly gets astride the wolf, then collars him by the ears, the hounds still holding on like grim death. Another *chasseur* then rides up, slips a muzzle on the wolf, which is then hauled on to one of the

rses, tightly strapped to the Mexican sort of saddle, and taken
f to a wagon in waiting near by. Foxes are similarly coursed
d killed with Foxhounds, the latter being stopped at the edge
'the covert.'

Such accounts hold considerable interest for the student of
e breed, and worthy of the portfolio is the story told by an
nglish army officer serving in Russia who saw Borzoi at work
Bielowicz. He himself had tried to hunt wolves with his fellow
fficers using Boarhounds, but the dogs had shown little prowess
t the sport, although even a big boar proved no problem to
em. A courier from a cuirassier regiment invited them to see
e Czar's wolfhounds at work and fine sport was promised,
e letter of invitation reading 'Don't trouble to bring any
eapons, for these are the dogs we have told you so much about,
nd they are to do all the work'. The *chasseur en chef* turned out
o be the man who for twenty years had charge of the Czar's
olfhounds. After a fine dinner, individual Borzoi were brought
n for inspection and although many dogs were recalcitrant at
eing dragged from their kennels, as soon as they saw the
hasseur they became 'as quiet as lambs', doing anything he
rdered. The man went over every dog, explaining its points,
virtues and accomplishments. One big dog Dimitri was reputed
able to catch and hold the largest wolf single-handed.

The next day (Lee reports) the description continues:

'As the coverts to be drawn were seven miles away, we took
an early start. Twelve *chasseurs*, each leading a fine wolfhound,
rode in advance; four attendants, with a pack of common
hounds followed. Next came an big iron cage, drawn by four,
horses, in which the captured wolves were to be put; for, while
small and inferior wolves are killed, all the largest are kept for
the young wolfhounds to practise upon. As soon as the common
hounds were sent into the underbush, hares and foxes came
rushing out, but the boars and wolves were harder to start. The
chasseurs had taken up good positions along the edge of the forest,
where a stretch of open plain offered a splendid chance to see
the fun if any wolves were driven out. I kept with the man who
had charge of Dimitri.

'With ears erect and nose in the air, this fine dog seemed to
take as much interest in the sport as any of us. Though the
barking and baying hounds in the coverts came nearer every
second, he never moved a muscle nor made a sound. Suddenly.
a big black wolf rushed out of the scrub, gave one glance
around, then started off for the next covert a mile away.

'All the dogs tugged at their leashes; but not till the wolf had
a clear start of two hundred yards did the head *chasseur*'s bugle
ring out. It was Dimitri's call; and as he was loosed he gave one
fierce howl and then bounded silently away.

'With such tremendous energy did he start that his feet hardly seemed to touch the ground. Every leap seemed longer than the last; and as he grew smaller in the distance, he looked like a big rubber ball bouncing over the plain, In less than a minute, he had overtaken the wolf and seized him by the neck under the right ear. A cloud of dust flew up as dog and wolf rolled over and over; but when it cleared away we saw that Dimitri had brought the beast to a standstill. His *chasseur* had followed him as quickly as his horse would run. On coming up the man jumped down, and getting astride the wolf, fastened a strong muzzle over its jaws, secured a chain round its neck and dragged the now skulking animal back to where the cage stood.

'In the meantime, other wolves had been started, and several of the dogs were hard at work. When two were loosed in pursuit of one wolf they ran alongside of him, one on each side, until a favourable opportunity offered, when, with a sudden snap, one would seize the creature. As the wolf turned to try to free himself, the other would get a grip that prevented him from moving at all. So surely and neatly did these dogs do their work that not one was bitten, although no animals can do quicker or more damaging work with their jaws than wolves.

'Seven wolves were driven out of that covert but only two were thought to be worth keeping. They were put in the cage, and we moved on to the next likely spot. In the course of the day the dogs caught sixteen wolves, not one got away when fairly out of cover, and we returned to the lodge with five fine live wolves.

'While discussing the ways of wolves that evening after dinner, one of us ventured to express a doubt whether even Dimitri could successfully face a wolf at bay. The speaker was satisfied that the dog could seize and hold a running wolf, but did not believe that he could avoid the savage attack such an animal makes when cornered. Before we left next morning he was convinced of his error. The largest captured wolf was turned loosed in an enclosed yard, and Dimitri was set upon him. Seeing himself trapped, the wolf did not wait for the dog to attack, but rushed straight at him. The two animals met and closed, rolling over and over; but when the struggles ceased Dimitri had the wolf securely by the neck, and had not received a scratch. Our friend, the *chasseur en chef*, offered to bring out other hounds that could do this feat as well as Dimitri; but we were convinced. As our time was up, we departed, regretting that we could not take a few of the Czar's wolfhounds away with us.'

The Borzoi in England

The breed was virtually unknown in England up to the end of the first half of the nineteenth century. Then, later on, as dog

shows began to achieve some popularity, the occasional
Siberian or Russian Wolfhound, as some Borzois were then
named, made its appearance. The type varied considerably,
however, due no doubt to many kinds which existed in Russia
and which had been quite freely interbred in some areas.

Mrs. W. Chadwick's Ch. Winjones Lebediska   *Photo: Fall*

The fact that the Prince of Wales (later to be Edward VII)
benefited from a gift by the Czar of Russia of two fine specimens
did much to enhance the breed's popularity. The names of
these two were 'Molodetz' and 'Owdalzka' and the Prince
exhibited them on a number of occasions, later using them for
breeding in conjunction with an addition to his kennel presented
by the Rev. J. C. Macdona, a cleric whose fancier interests
extended to many breeds. At a dog show in 1871, a foreign
variety class which was arranged to satisfy a number of

exhibitors was well-supported by 'Russian' hounds, Mr. S. T. Holland's 'Tom' winning the first prize against strong competition comprised of Lady Emily Peel's home-bred white-and-lemon 'Czar' and the aforementioned Rev. Macdona's 'Sandringham'. However, it is to 'Sultan', described as a 'Russian' Wolfhound to whom the credit for being the first Borzoi exhibited in England must go. He appeared at the First Great International Show of Sporting and other Dogs, 25th–30th May, 1863, at the Agricultural Hall, Islington, London. Owned by the Duchess of Manchester, he was a big hound, standing 31 inches at the shoulders and very powerfully built. Bred by Prince William of Prussia, he was aged nearly five years and priced to sell at £1000. Unfortunately, he was beaten at the show by a 'North German Boar Hound' called 'Juba', also the property of the Duchess of Manchester. This lady must have participated in some unusual breeds for the period for in the same year she won a prize with her 'Katae', described as a 'Fan-tailed Greyhound'!

Some twenty years later than the above events Lady Charles Kerr founded her kennels. Lee reports that the inmates were 'small and somewhat light and weedy'. Even then the name 'Borzoi' which means 'swift' was not in general use, the term 'Russian Wolfhound' seemingly being preferred by most owners and even chosen to name the breed in America. However, as the delightful Asiatic hounds became increasingly popular, so did the generic name 'Borzoi' become more acceptable to the dog world of the day. Gradually, such appellations as 'Fan-tailed Greyhounds', 'Circassian Orloff Wolfhounds' and 'Siberian Greyhounds/Wolfhounds' were being dispensed with, and Borzoi breeding as such became better established. In 1890, the Duchess of Newcastle who was to be one of the breed's greatest pillars commenced exhibiting. The show was the Kennel Club event of that year and she exhibited a litter by a dog named 'Ivan II', bought in Paris out of her mother's former bitch 'Spain', a gift from a Spanish Marquis some years earlier. It was not long ere the 'of Notts' kennel was founded at Clumber and stocked with magnificent Borzois, regardless of expense. Some of the earlier dogs, especially were stated to have been superb, including Mr. Muir's white and lemon 'Krilutt', Col. Wellesley's white and blue 'Korotai', a dog who had been proven at wolf-hunting in his native Russia. 'Oudar', a male of 30½ inches at the shoulder weighing 105 lb. and 'Oosslad', a fawn. This dog was perceptibly smaller than his companions, but finely made in head. The Duchess herself referred to 'Oudar', in a letter to Henry Compton, author of *The Twentieth-Century Dog*, 1904, claiming that he and his litter brother and two sisters were the best among some twenty specimens brought to England in 1892 by Mr. Cremiere on the instructions of the

Grand Duke Nicholas. 'Oudar's' purchase price was said to be £200. These specimens did much to lay good foundations for the breed in Britain. The 'of Notts' establishment at one time held no less than one hundred Borzois, although Lee is more conservative and states the figure was nearer fifty. The Duchess of Newcastle, although she never judged the breed until 1948 was an acknowledged Borzoi expert. Her letter to Compton, written before 1904, deplored the fact that many were becoming too light-eyed, and breeders were putting size before depth of chest and getting sides which were too flat. She believed the British specimens were generally sounder than those to be found in Russia, commenting that this may well have been due to our less severe winter.

Of course, a number of other enthusiasts contributed substantially to the Borzoi's success in the show ring and to his welfare in breeding, but it is not the purpose of this book to list owners other than the very early name or two, so as to give an idea as to the circles in which the Borzoi moved when his breed career commenced in England. There is little doubt that he owes much of his successful impact on the British to his association with the royalty and noble families of the land who could afford to sponsor him.

In 1895, the Princess of Wales, later to be the Queen, received from the Czar's kennels, *via* a Mr. Rousseau, a Borzoi whose name was to become famous. As a dog, he was to popularize his breed, not only in royal affections, but in the heart of the British public. This was the immortal 'Alex', who won a good deal, probably no less than one hundred first prizes in his career, having the distinction of participating in top honours for the Kennel Club Championship in 1900, but dying in 1902. In 1905, the Queen's 'Vassilka' won the championship in strong competition, an award which we learn was well received by the onlookers.

The Borzoi Club

The Borzoi Club was founded in March 1892 with the Duke and Duchess of Newcastle as joint presidents. Its objects are to promote the breeding of pure Borzois by endeavouring to make the qualities and type of the breed better known. The Club holds an annual show in conjunction with a noted all-breed championship show event. It is well endowed with valuable trophies to be competed for, the original two Borzoi Club Challenge Cups being of especial interest. One is awarded for best dog in show and the other for best bitch. These are magnificent cups in sterling silver standing 20 inches high being first challenged for in 1896, the Duchess of Newcastle winning them. Another much sought-after trophy is the Bleriot Challenge

Bowl, presented to the Borzoi Club by Mr. Louis Bleriot, the airman, in 1913. It was won in the same year by Mrs. Borman. All Borzoi owners and enthusiasts should join this progressive body. Members keep abreast of events in the breed, attend shows sponsored by the club and have the opportunity to mix socially and with advantage at meetings and discussion groups when held. There exists always an opportunity for expert and novice alike to learn more of this beautiful and sporting hound. For further information write to the efficient honorary secretary:

> Mrs. Eileen E. Ruggles,
> 'Matalona' Borzois,
> Maldon Hall,
> Spital Road, MALDON,
> Essex.
> Telephone: Maldon 3998.

It should be noted that the above is the name and address of the current honorary secretary. However, the office is one which in many clubs change annually. Should you be unable to contact the lady named, you are advised to write to the Secretary, The Kennel Club, 1–4 Clarges Street, Piccadilly, London, W1Y 8AB, asking to be put in touch with an active officer of the Borzoi Club. Those who seek information about the various overseas Borzoi clubs and associations should apply to the Kennel Club of the country concerned.

Winjones Borzois, 1952. *L. to R.*: Winjones Ermolai, W. Astral, W. Lohodka, Ch. W. Lebediska, W. Kalinka (exported to Australia), Ch. W. Naljot, W. Dunyashka, W. Naglaty (exported to Australia)

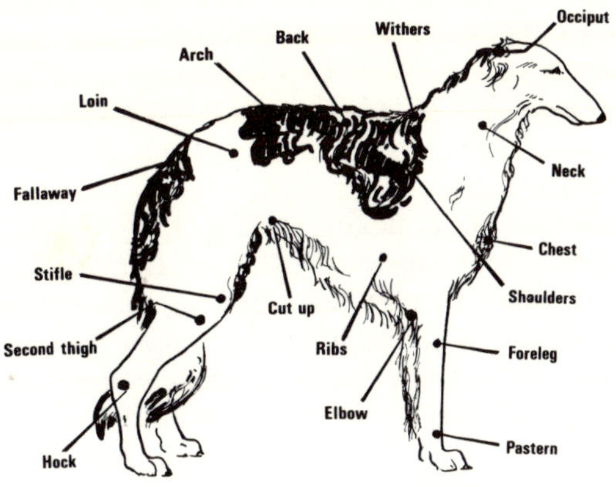

Chapter 2

The British Standard

THE wording of the Borzoi Standard as we know it in Britain is basically the same as that used in other countries, with the exception of the U.S.S.R. where it reads more descriptively and detailed (see pp. 26–8).

The Borzoi Club revised our Standard in 1922 at a general meeting. It is as follows:

General Appearance: Very graceful, aristocratic and elegant, combining courage, muscular power and great speed.

Head and Skull: Head, long and lean. Well filled in below the eyes. Measurement equal from the occiput to the inner corner of the eye, and from the inner corner of the eye to tip of nose. Skull very slightly domed and narrow, stop not perceptible, inclining to Roman nose. Head fine so that the direction of the bones and principal veins can be clearly seen. Bitches' heads should be finer than dogs'. Jaws long, deep and powerful; nose large and black, not pink or brown, nicely rounded, neither cornered nor sharp. Viewed from above should look narrow, converging very gradually to tip of nose.

Eyes: Dark, intelligent, alert and keen. Almond shaped, set obliquely, placed well back, but not too far apart. Eye rims dark. Eyes should not be light, round or staring.

Ears: Small and fine in quality; not too far apart. They should be active and responsive; when alert can be erect; when in response nearly touching at the occiput.

Mouth: Teeth even, neither pig-jawed nor undershot.

MOUTHS

(a) **Undershot. The lower incisors project beyond the upper incisors with a space between. Faulty.**

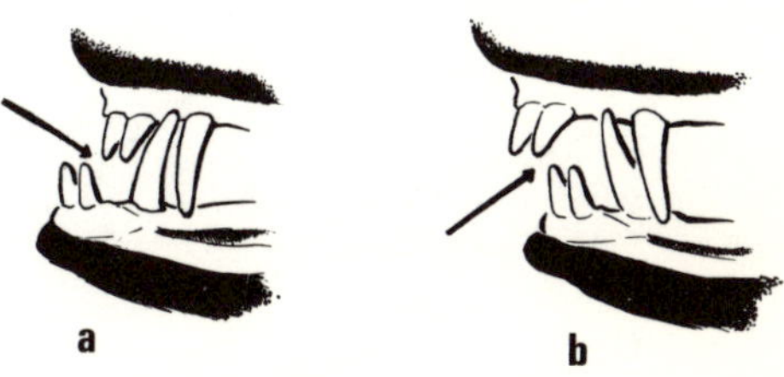

(b) **Overshot. The upper incisors protrude beyond the lower incisors with a space between. Faulty.**

(c) **Level Mouth. The upper incisors rest over and upon the lower incisors when the mouth is closed. Correct.**

15

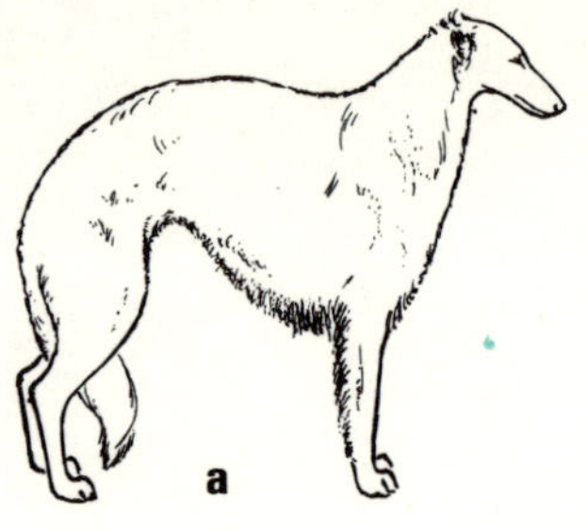

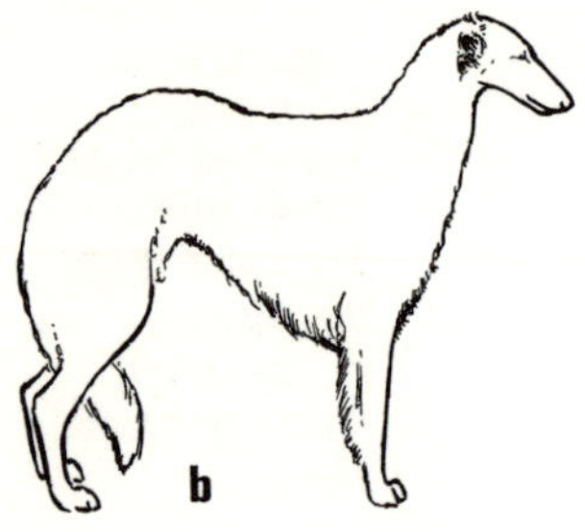

**TOPLINES
AND
SIDES**

(a) Typical.

**(b) Arch starts too
far back and
'humped'.**

**(c) Ewe neck. Does
not 'flow' into
back. Straight
topline.**

Neck: Clean, slightly arched, reasonably long, powerful. Well set on, free from throatiness. Flat at the sides, not round.

Forequarters: Shoulders clean, sloping well back, fine at withers, free from lumpiness. Fore legs lean and straight. Seen from the front, narrow like blades; from the side, wide at shoulder, narrowing down to foot; elbows turned neither in, nor out; pasterns strong, flexible and springy.

Body: Chest, great depth of brisket, rather narrow. Ribs well sprung and flexible; neither flat sided nor barrel-shaped. Very deep, giving heart room and lung play, especially in the case of mature males. (It is from depth of chest rather than breadth that the Borzoi derives its heart room and lung play.) Back rising in a graceful arch from as near the shoulder as possible with a well-balanced fall-away. The arch to be more marked in dogs than bitches. Rather bony, muscular and free from any cavity. Muscles highly developed and well distributed.

Hindquarters: Loins broad and very powerful, with plenty of muscular development. Quarters should be wider than shoulders, ensuring stability of stance. Thighs long, well developed with good second thigh. Hind legs long, muscular, stifles well bent, hocks broad, clean and well let down.

Feet: Front feet rather long, toes close together; well arched, never flat, neither turning in nor out. Hind feet hare-like, i.e. longer and less arched.

Tail: Long, rather low set. Well feathered, carried low, not gaily. In action may be used as rudder but not rising above level of the back. From the level of the hocks may be sickle shaped but not ringed.

Coat: Long and silky (never woolly), or flat, or wavy or rather curly. Short and smooth on head, ears and front of legs, on neck the frill profuse and rather curly, fore legs and chest well feathered, on hindquarters and tail, long and profuse.

Size: Height at shoulder: Dogs from 29 inches upwards; Bitches from 27 inches upwards.

The Borzoi Standard, as per pp. 9–10 of the Kennel Club Standards of the Breeds, Sporting, Z(1), is reproduced with kind permission of the Kennel Club.

In 1922, the Borzoi Club at a general meeting, discussed the breed Standard and recommended the following matter to be incorporated with the official wording:

Characteristics: Alertness, dignity and courage.

Colour: Immaterial. In the opinion of the Club, a dog should never be penalized for being self-coloured.

Faults: Short neck, coarse, and big ears. 'Dish-faced', coarse head, light or round eyes, straight shoulders, flat back, arch starting too far back, too narrow in front. Round bone, straight hocks, weak quarters, coarse coat, splay footed, too close behind, also lack of quality and lack of condition.

Observations on the British Standard

The British Kennel Club Standard you have just read is the 'Standard of Excellence' as it applies to the Borzoi and is the reference by which Borzois are currently judged. At one time, there was a Scale of Points issued with the Standard and this purported to help judges. Unfortunately, these did little more than to confuse them! Judging by an arbitrary system of points is not really feasible and the method is not approved today either officially or by the breed itself. In fact, it has no merit other than to give the judge or fancier an extremely rough guide. The Scale of Points is given below more for its antique interest than anything else. These are as declared at the Borzoi Club's 1922 meeting.

	Points Values
Head complete (eyes and ears included)	15
Neck	10
Shoulders and Chest	15
Ribs, Back and Loins	15
Hindquarters, Stifles and Hocks	15
Legs and Feet	15
Coat, Tail and Feather	10
General Appearance	5
Total:	100

To understand the Standard of the breed you need to read and study it in conjunction with a first-class living specimen Borzoi to whom you can refer. A good judge of the breed needs to have owned a good specimen or two at some time or other of his career in the Fancy. Otherwise, it is doubtful if he can truly appreciate and understand the physical virtues, characteristics and worth of a Borzoi. When you have an excellent specimen running around your home and person, his type, form, substance, temperament and gait all become impressed upon your subsconscious. Then when you judge, these impressions will be projected on to the dogs standing before you in the ring. Admittedly, you need to be flexible enough in your mind to realize that you cannot compare too rigidly dogs from other strains and other kennels with dogs (however good) that you have owned. You must perforce, allow some leeway in the matter of finer points, otherwise your judgement would quickly

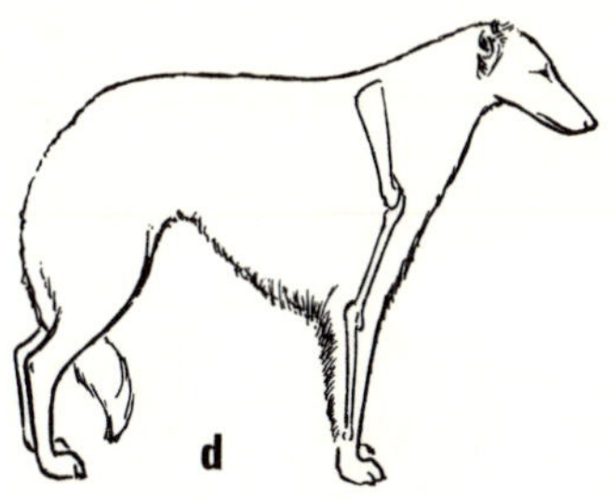

(d) Perpendicular shoulder formation causing head to be thrust forward. Flat topline.

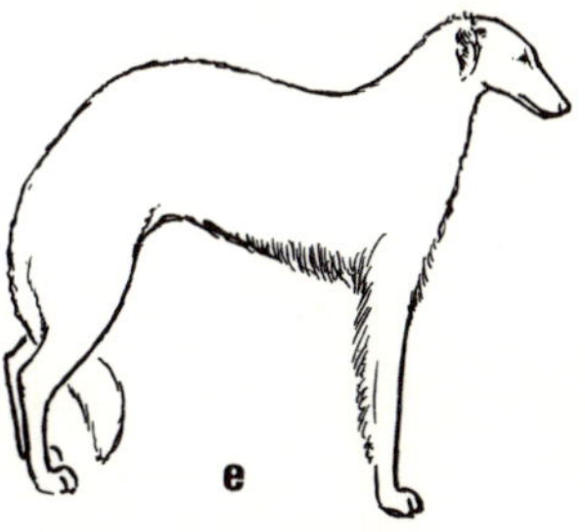

(e) Lacking depth of chest; shallow brisket; shelly; too long in couplings.

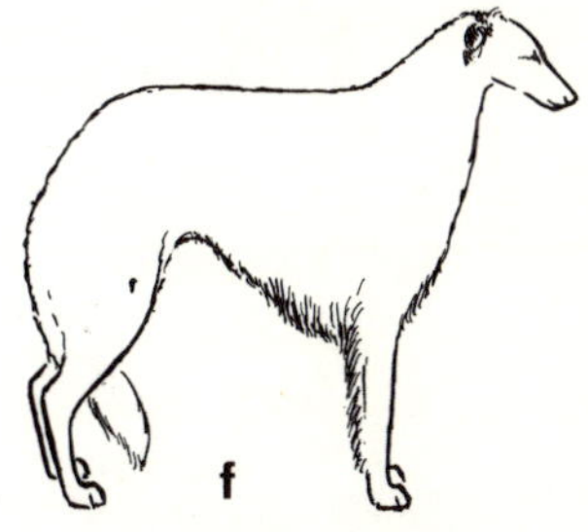

(f) Straight topline; 'fall-away' too sudden.

17

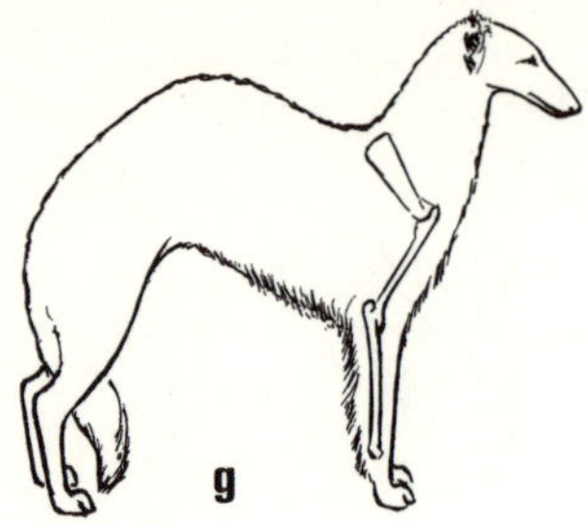

(g) Scapula short inducing dip at withers and too arched over loins.

become biased. However, it must be remembered that there is only *one* type of Borzoi wanted and that is the *correct* type.

The Standard is intended as a *Guide* only. It is probably not detailed enough to be much more than this and yet really it needs no more detail! A dog (in any breed) needs to be judged as a whole. Too much detail causes confusion and permits so often unimportant points to be weighed strongly and wrongly against features which are genuinely important. The Standard was evolved and written by experts who knew what a *real* Borzoi should look like, emphasizing the features which they insisted should be perpetuated. The breed Standard is a target at which all conscientious breeders aim and have been aiming at for many generations of breeding because they have found it a good and reliable term of reference in their search for the perfect specimen. The fact that Borzois are today handsome, elegant hounds with the stamp of high pedigree set upon them, probably more than in most breeds, speaks for the worth and workability of the Standard. It indicates too, the importance of letting the present Standard remain unaltered. Change it and the breed is put into a state of some confusion, possibly only of a temporary nature, but causing a situation likely to cause disheartenment and disinterest in its ranks. The fact is that the present-day Standard has proved itself a competent one and has been instrumental over the last ninety years in more or less similar form in Britain in building up the type and temperament of the breed we know today. This in itself is enough to justify its retention.

Mrs. W. Chadwick's Ch. Winjones Razluka and Winjones Scandal of Fortrouge

Understanding the Standard

No two people will read and 'understand' the Standard identically. It is best to treat the written Standard as a sort of 'blueprint' describing the *perfect* Borzoi. That anyone has ever seen such a paragon is open to doubt. Even the best dogs in the breed (or any breed for that matter) are unlikely to reach a Standard of worth of 75 per cent. Bearing this in mind, it suggests that there remains plenty of room still for Borzois to improve and attain perfection, at least.

In all breeds (and Borzois are no exception) there exist faddists. Faddists seek specific and preferred points to develop in their strains. Head beauty, of course, is always a prime desideratum and a worthy one too, for it is the 'hallmark' of the Borzoi, but if it is bred for and developed regardless of other points, just as vital, especially temperamental ones, then it must be a badly conceived system of breeding. Exaggeration in the development of breed points is a bad thing, too, and beware of the breeder who tries to shape the Standard to fit his dog rather than the reverse.

Here then are some observations on the various points of the Standard:

General Appearance

This is the way a dog presents himself and by which impression he is initially assessed. He *must*, if he is to gain high marks in this section, have type. This means good breed type, of course, and it means real quality and pedigree nobility in his appearance. This is essential in a dog if he is to epitomize the ideal model of his breed, based on the description imparted by the breed Standard. You can usually recognize good type when you see it, but it often happens that some typey dogs are unsound. You can have a Borzoi with all his body components individually well typed so that standing he makes what a judge would term a 'perfect picture'. But get that dog to move and at once all his virtue falls away and it becomes clear that although the parts are excellent, they are not fused together in a proper and pleasing fashion. The dog is in effect unsound and because he is unsound he becomes suspect immediately as a breeding proposition. The linkage between his parts are faulty, i.e. no one part is joined soundly and effectively to another. His head might well be ideal, his body too, yet the head is associated with the body by a neck (probably good as necks go) in an untidy, somehow irrelevant manner. His hindquarters, although well made and beautifully muscled go down to feet which by the loose way they link might well belong to another Borzoi entirely! This lack of physical integration is unsoundness, worse it is transmittable in breeding. Such dogs are invariably quite useless to the serious breeder with a future strain in mind. From a perfect picture standing the Borzoi becomes, when moved, an unsound specimen; this showing just how important it is to see a dog in action before commenting on its worth. In effect, type *must* be complemented by complete soundness. Satisfaction rests somewhere between the two necessities and the degree can vary considerably depending on the specimen under review for it is controlled by the relative worth of his respective physical points as applied to the Borzoi Standard.

A Borzoi to fulfil his breed requirements in the matter of general appearance should reveal in his pedigree nobility, already referred to—alertness, dignity and courage as demanded officially for his characteristics. That his poise, gait and stance should be graceful, regal, elegant and reveal a hound capable of great speed and strength we are apprized. This means that his balance must be correct, his outline classical and deportment without fault. Balance is contributed to by co-ordination between the body structure and the muscle distribution, and if it is good, it means that when seen from any angle the effect is a pleasing one without exaggeration in any department.

Head and Skull

The head is probably the Borzoi's most important feature. At one time breeders (as in the Bull Terrier fancy) developed it to such an extent that the dog's other parts were almost forgotten. Many hounds were being produced possessing wonderful heads and what might be termed 'hooped' backs, little else! This sad state of affairs was rectified and today the Borzoi is a good all-round dog both physically and mentally.

HEADS

(a) Dish Face.

(b) Ill-formed Roman nose.

(c) Typical forward balance.

(d) Weak 'snipy' muzzle.

(e) Showing 'stop'.

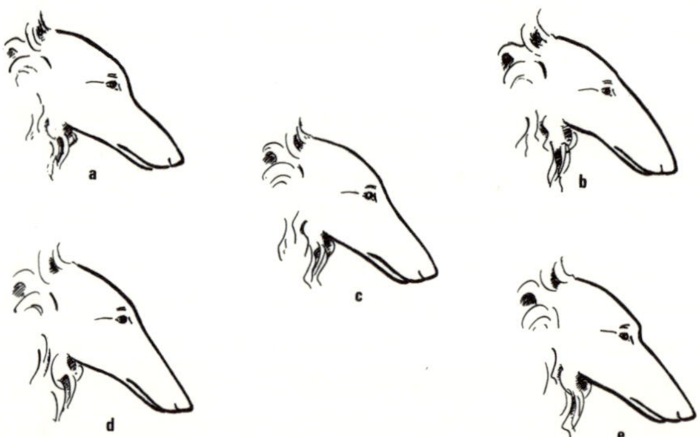

The Borzoi's head must show his strength and beauty and it must never be forgotten that it has to remain built and capable to take and grip a wolf. This means that the head's great length must be maintained with adequate depth, the foreface and muzzle forming more than half the entire length of the skull. The sagittal crest should be well developed, and there should be plenty of fill-up before the eyes with a perceptible Roman nose finish, although the latter feature must not be exaggerated.

It is important that a dog should look masculine and his female counterpart should evince her femininity. This might appear obvious, but it often occurs that a dog by virtue of his excessive refinement will seem 'bitchy' and a bitch by her coarseness appear 'doggy'. Both are faults, the former the more detestable.

Eyes

The colour of the eyes is important. The dark eye is always preferable to a light one. The former evinces intelligence, the latter shrewdness while a nice dark eye lends itself at once to the Borzoi's correct expression and outlook, playing its part in the matters of general appearance. Eye emplacement and shape must never be overlooked. A round eye just as an eye set too far forward will give an alien expression to the hound and detract considerably from his general worth.

Ears

The Borzoi's ears should be small and of fine texture and when laid back should nearly touch at the occiput where it joins the neck's upper end. Ears should always be responsive to sound and vibration for they contribute towards the hound's verve and expression, especially important in the show ring. Ears which are set on too low or otherwise badly placed completely detract from these factors.

Mouth

The Borzoi's mouth should be 'level', i.e. with the upper jaw incisors resting over and upon the incisors of the lower jaw with no space between. Bad mouth formations which include the undershot jaw, i.e. with the incisors of the lower jaw protruding beyond those of the upper jaw (as in the Bulldog) and the overshot mouth which has the upper incisors projecting beyond the teeth in the lower jaw with a space between them are quite objectionable. The latter is sometimes known as 'pig-jaw'. Perfect mouth formation is of considerable importance. To neglect it leaves the way open for narrow jaws with missing and small teeth, quite wrong in a strong coursing breed like the Borzoi. The adult dog should have a quota of teeth as follows:

	Upper Jaw	Lower Jaw
Cutting Teeth (Incisors)	6	6
Tusks or Eye Teeth (Canines)	2	2
Premolars	8	8
Grinding Teeth (Molars)	4	6
	20	22

The last upper pre-molars and first lower pre-molars are used for tearing flesh. They are called carnassials and have to be extremely strong. Their absence in some breeds has been noted and this may be a hereditary weakness which needs watching in dogdom.

Neck

The line of the neck's crest or mane should be a firm, graceful curve. It should be rather long, the cervical vertebrae fusing smoothly into the dorsal vertebrae through the withers. The neck is important for it must carry the head high in a dignified and regal manner and at the same time administer the armament of the Borzoi's head when he strikes contact with his quarry. The set of the neck is dependent on the shoulders and upright shoulders will cause it to thrust forward and out with the head placed in too low a position. The Borzoi's neck should be 'clean', i.e. free from throatiness caused by too much skin under the jaw line.

Forequarters

The front should be straight and positive, the fore legs amply boned but lean and straight. The forequarters take the Borzoi's body-weight at speed, whereas the fore legs and fore feet contribute in directing the dog. The actual weight taken is probably more than half the hound's body-weight when he is at full gallop and the articulation between the lower end of the scapula (shoulder-blade) and the upper end of the humerus (arm bone) should be angled in such a way as to form a sort of shock-absorber against any jarring impact to which the hound would be subject.

The formation of the front is especially important in a hound whose nature it is to hunt by sight, i.e. a member of the gaze-hound family. The fore limbs are brought forward in a positive manner, contributing in part to the animal's propulsion, although not to the same extent as do the hind limbs. A Borzoi gallops with his head held high, his quarry kept in full sight, quite the reverse to a dog whose function it is to track by scent alone. Because the Borzoi's neck muscles are rigidly contracted

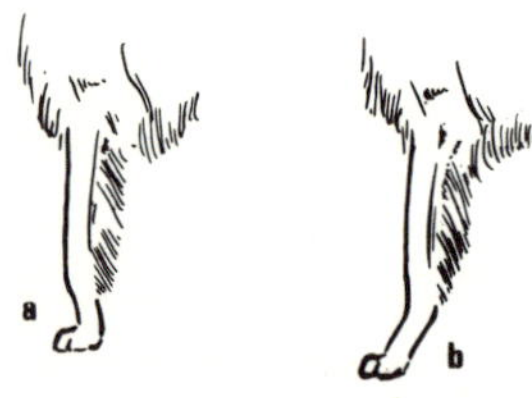

FORELEGS

(a) **Weakness at knee; foot thrown to rear.**

(b) **Weak pastern; foot thrown forward.**

in this exercise, the reach of his fore feet is allowed full play. However, this reach cannot advance much beyond an imaginary line extended down to the ground from the spine of the scapula. This means that the more laid back the shoulder-blade, the more advance permitted the dog's fore legs, which will result in the greater stride and speed of the hound in the chase. The elbows should lie well into the sides of the chest; if they jut out ('out at elbow') the fore feet will turn in ('pin-toed') and completely mar the hound's action and militate against his staying power.

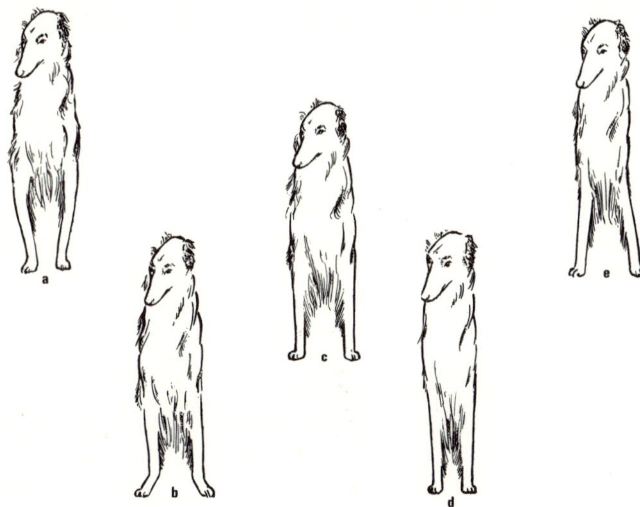

FRONTS

(a) **Bowed front.**

(b) **Weak at pasterns forefeet turnout.**

(c) **Good breadth of front, but lacking elegance in stance.**

(d) **Front tight and narrow.**

(e) **Chest tight; Forefeet thrown apart.**

The tops of the shoulder-blades should be well laid back with not too much width between them at their highest point where they are set against the dorsal vertebrae. The lower end of the scapula, articulating with the upper end of the humerus should form an acute angle thereby allowing easy and free action when the hound moves. If the angle so made is an obtuse one the shoulders are said to be upright and no coursing hound can function properly with such a formation which would render his gait stilted, almost mincing. Further, a big dog such as the Borzoi with so much body-weight on his foreparts, because they lack resilience, is inclined to throw out his elbows under pressure. This is how unsound fronts are produced.

Body

The dorsal vertebrae which makes up the Borzoi's back is composed of thirteen connected bony segments. From each of these spring a pair of ribs, nine of these extending downwards to join with the sternum or breastbone. These are termed 'true' ribs the remaining four being not so attached are called 'false' the last being floating ribs.

HINDLEGS

(a) Straight stifle. Upright hock joint.

(b) Over-angulation of hind limb.

Victoria de Quincey's Veedeque's Adrian of Greenhaven

Courtesy Sheffield Morning Telegraph

The rib-cage houses and protects the dog's heart and lungs, the ideal formation of the ribs being well sprung and rounded, not barrelled. The ribs should be of considerable length in order to produce a deep chest and the deeper this the better. As a guide, the minimum depth required should be seen as a line to the 'keel' passing through the point of elbow. However, one must avoid any tendency towards breeding for false depth. This would involve the development of extra cartilage around the sternum instead of providing more room above it. A hound bred in this way would be ill-served in the field. The chest should be only moderately broad, coarseness militating severely against the Borzoi's free movement. The ribs, too, should never show broad and coarse across the back, for the coursing hound family is made on sleeker lines for speed and easy action.

The dorsal vertebrae, which is 'built up' a little with bony formation is continued towards the hound's rear end with the seven lumbar bones of the spinal column, followed by the sacrum which is a triangular bony process where the tail is set on. The all-important arch of the Borzoi's loins takes place over the area of the loins, although its curve commences just behind the third vertebrae. This arch allows the Borzoi to gather himself up for added speed and the lightning switching of direction in the chase for which he is so noted. Correct degree of arching commencing from just behind the shoulder with beauty and balance in the curve and the resultant fall-away at croup are features to be given perfection and preserved. Not only do they contribute to the hound's function in sport, but in the fulfilment of the points he can earn in the ring.

Hindquarters

The hindquarters must be well muscled and immensely strong, the loins in particular being very broad and powerful. The propulsion they provide the Borzoi is dependent on the angulation and muscular development in this region, directed through the pelvis. The thighs should be well endowed with long, strong muscles. Long muscles are 'lasting' muscles permitting stamina in the field. Bunched or 'knotted' muscles, although very strong tire easily and never lend themselves to the lithe, free and easy action expected in this breed of hound. The angle made by the first or upper thigh bone (*femur*) and the second or lower thigh bone (*tibia*) decides the quality of the stifle joint on which good action depends. Both thighs must be strongly muscled and padded with cartilage and ligaments. Often, a big breed, used to exerting itself to the full, will put considerable stress on to these ligaments and stretch them, causing lameness. This can prove chronic if ignored and all coursing hounds need close attention at the first signs of any unsoundness. A dog with a wide or obtuse angle at the stifle is said to be 'straight in stifle'. His gait will be stilted and this will reduce considerably his stamina and ability to propel himself with the power and speed expected of him. It is important to avoid straight-stifled Borzois in breeding plans for the fault is transmittable in breeding. A well-bent stifle is said to be highly desirable* and to be sought for and bred to always. Seen from the rear the Borzoi's hind legs should be straight and set down firmly and squarely. From the side, the hound's hocks should be well angulated and the feet placed slightly behind the perpendicular and seemingly ready for the 'off'.

Feet

The Borzoi's feet should be well knit and well arched. They must not turn either in or out and be well padded. Flat and splayed feet will never allow the dog to move with characteristic speed and spring, for they are due to slack muscles and tendon. This is why a youngster's exercise should always be conducted on hard ground such as cinder paths, for grass has a deleterious effect on the feet of a heavy breed particularly. The pasterns should be strong and firm, showing no signs of weakness.

Tail

The Borzoi's tail can often make or mar him in the matter of

** I believe the Russians are less than adamant on this point and are inclined to view it as an aesthetic feature not necessarily calculated to aid a good coursing hound. Author.*

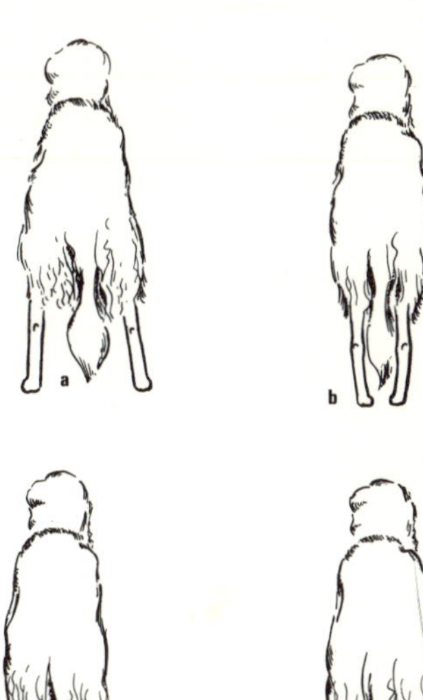

HIND-QUARTERS

(a) **Hindlegs inclined to 'spread'.**

(b) **Hocks turned out; feet in-turned.**

(c) **Cow-hocks; feet turned out.**

(d) **Typical.**

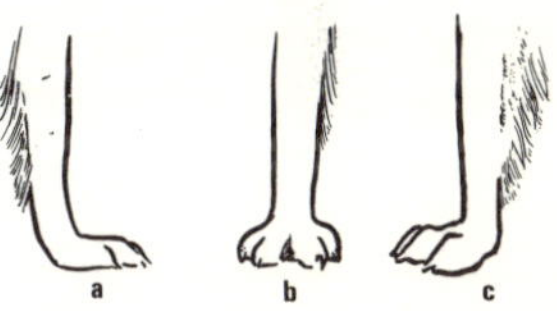

FEET

(a) **Flat, weak foot.**

(b) **Splayed foot.**

(c) **Typical.**

general appearance. The set-on is all important and should be rather low so that it cannot be held in an over-elevated position. On the other hand, a tail too low set will be dragged or held flaccidly quite unattractively. No one likes a tail which is ringed and a nice sickle-curve from hock level is preferred. As in the Irish Wolfhound, the Borzoi uses his tail as a rudder in the chase and good feathering then becomes an added asset.

Coat

From the very early days in the breed when Borzois were known in their various forms and types and coats differed from short to long, flat to curly the modern Borzoi's adornment is one of beauty. The Standard's wording is quite specific and needs no amplification.

Size

It is important to maintain size in a breed such as the Borzoi. Dogs of many breeds are gradually getting smaller, more is the pity. A hound bred for hunting the wolf needs to be a big, powerful animal. We must keep in mind the Borzoi's original purpose and breed dogs which seem likely to conform both in physique and temperament to that sport's requirements. Weight and size seem always to represent controversial discussion matter in canine circles and opinions vary considerably. However, it is clear that if the dog is to be big then his weight must increase accordingly and a balance assessed visually, will perhaps determine the spread of weight for size, or *vice versa*.

The Russian Standard of the Borzoi

The Russian Borzoi breed Standard is, as might be expected, a very detailed and descriptive document. It should be published because much can be learned from it. The translation from the Russian was effected by Miss Ursula-v. Trueb of Switzerland, to whom many thanks.

As a breed, the Psovaya Barzaya of today derives from the old Russian Coursing Hound with a light contribution of Crimean and Mountain (Caucasus) Hound blood.

Area of distribution: Wood covered steppes and steppes of the European part of the Soviet Union, Georgia and Siberia.

The Psovaya Barzaya had the following hunting characteristics: Sharp sight, great speed, mainly on short distances, keenness towards game and great strength.

General Appearance, Type of Construction, Movement: Hound of great height, long racy build and strong. The height at the withers is of 70–82 centimetres ($27\frac{1}{4}$–$32\frac{1}{2}$ inches for males, about 5 centimetres less for bitches. The height at the withers is almost the same as that of the croup or hardly superior. The length index is about 105 for males, about 107 for bitches.

Temperament: Quiet.

Characteristic Movement: Until the game is raised, a not very fast trot; during the chase a speedy gallop in long, fleet leaps.

Colours: White; sable of all shades; silver shaded sable, dark shaded sable; tan shade with black, muzzle and legs dark; grey, from ash-grey to yellowish-grey; brindled, sable or tan or grey with extended darker stripes; tan, black and all intermediary shades of these colours. Tan points are admissible but not desired.

For dark-coloured dogs, a black muzzle is typical as well as dark patches on the body.

All colours can be either plain or spotted.

The self-coloured dogs are darker on the upper side, the colour fading into a lighter shade towards the extremities, the belly and the hind part of the legs.

Coat: The hair is soft, wavy or in great curls. At the head and legs the hair is short. At the neck, on the back and on the breast, the hair is longer. The ornamental hair is most developed around the neck, at the lower part of the chest, the belly, the hind part of the front legs and the thighs. At the lower part of the tail it hangs in fringes; at the upper part of the tail, it is curly.

Skin, Muscles, Bone: The skin is thin, elastic, without any loose cellular tissue underneath and without folds. The muscles are strongly developed, long. The bones are solid.

Head: Long, narrow, lean. The length of the muzzle is equal to that of the skull. The passage from the forehead to the muzzle is hardly noticeable. Seen from the side, forehead and upper line of muzzle form an almost straight line, very slightly convex. The skull is narrow, oval-shaped. The occipital hillock is well accentuated. The upper part of the skull is straight or receding.

Muzzle: Narrow, straight, lean, with a slight hill towards the nose. The nose is black, over-reaching. The lips are thin, well stretched along the jaw bones, with dark rims.

Ears: Small, delicate, narrow, pointed, set high, not very far apart, folded back along the neck, the tips very close together. When alert, the Psovaya Barzaya raises the ears on their cartilages, the tips sometimes falling over.

Eyes: Large, the lids cut obliquely, dark-brown or chestnut-brown. The lids are black.

Neck: Long, slightly arched, well muscled, flattened laterally, set at an angle of 50–60° to the longitudinal axis of the body.

Chest: Not broad, of narrow oval, reaching to the elbows and lower. The ribs are regular, getting shorter towards the rear part of the chest which goes sharply over to the belly.

Withers: Not pronounced.

Back: Wide, muscled, slightly arched, forming a regular arch prolonged by the loins. This arch is more pronounced in males than in bitches.

Loins: Strong, muscular, not accentuated.

Croup: Long, wide, muscled, with a slight fall-down. The width between the hip-bones must be at least 8 cm.

Belly: Sharply tucked-up. The passage from the false-ribs to the belly is very accentuated.

Forequarters: Straight, lean, bony, muscled. Seen from the front, the legs are straight and parallel. The shoulders are muscled. The bones are oval cut. The elbows are directed to the rear. The shoulder-angle is of about 110–120°. The length of the fore legs is nearly equal to half of the total height at the withers. The pasterns are slightly bent.

Hindquarters: Lean, bony, muscled. Seen from the back, the legs are straight and parallel. Seen from the side, they show well developed angles of the joints. They are wide standing and slightly pulled to the rear. The thighs are well developed with jutting-out muscles. The angle of the hock is lean, slightly rounded at the rear; the hocks are short, vertical.

Feet: Lean, narrow, of oval shape, with slightly arched toes. The nails touch the ground.

Tail: Sabre or slightly sickle shaped, tapering, with heavy feathering. When the dog is quiet, the tail is hanging; when he is excited, it should not be carried above the top-line of the back. Long. Pulled between the thighs, it should reach the top of the nearest hip-bone.

Mrs. W. Chadwick's Ch. Winjones Naljot and Ch. Winjones Lebediska

Faults and Insufficiencies of the Psovaya Barzaya

General Appearance, Type of Construction: Too high on the legs, too long, short on the legs, height less than the given measures.

Colours: Too sharply accentuated tan points; coffee-coloured; speckled.

Coat: Dull, short hair, ruffled, little furnished; insufficient development of the hair at the thighs and of the feathering; hard, dense and equally distributed on the whole body.

Head: Pronounced passage from the skull to the muzzle; clumsy; too broad in cheeks; snipey muzzle; light coloured nose.

Ears: Set low, too wide apart, not enough drawn back and close to the neck, large, clumsy, with rounded tips.

Eyes: Small, round opening of lids; light coloured eyes; light lids.

Neck: Round, clumsy.

Chest: Narrow, hollow, too broad.

Back: Narrow, sunken, a saddle-back is a heavy fault. A flat back is a fault for males, an insufficience for bitches.

Mr. R. Duckworth's Sholwood's Seraph and Seraphine *Photo: Gibbs*

Croup: Narrow, insufficient.

Belly: Not enough tuck-up. Too long.

Forequarters: Weak pasterns; close or loose elbows; out-turned feet; irregular clumsy moving, signs of rickets.

Hindquarters: Cow-hocked; O-shaped; not enough accentuated angle of hock; too straight rear; too thick feet.

Feet: Spread toes; thick, round feet.

Tail: Short, ring-shaped, carried high; not enough feathering.

All imperfections have to be considered as faults or insufficiencies, depending on the degree of their accentuation.

Mrs. J. L. Gibbs' Ch. Galina of Colhugh and Opal of Fortrouge sporting in the snow
Photo: Gibbs

The 'Boldareff' Description

It is of interest to read from *The Stock Keeper* (July) 1896, an article on the Borzoi translated from the Russian by a member of the Imperial Hunt, M. A. Boldareff. It reads:

'The general appearance of the Borzoi is noble and elegant. This is shown in the shape of the head, the silkiness and brilliancy of the hair, and even in the gait, which should be full of energy and grace. The different points of the dog, taken separately, have no value in the general appearance; the dog may have defects in head properties, in the body, in the legs, the coat may be too short, but nevertheless its air of nobility and elegance, its blue-blood aspect, will indicate purity of breeding. Only pure blood and the most careful breeding for several generations will impart this look, which excites the admiration of connoisseurs of Borzoi, and all other lovers of dogs.

'It is a pity that nowadays many of our sportsmen surrender general appearance for perfection in other points, so that the Borzoi of high and noble quality is becoming rare.

'The pure race of Borzoi is principally characterized by the shape of the head, the ear, and by the tail. Many breeders concentrate their attention upon the head, and disdain the tail.

'We find, on the contrary, that the tail is one of the most characteristic points of race, because its thinness, its elasticity, and its shape, which resembles a reaping hook (*a*) among all the Russian breeds (we consider the Crimean and Caucasian varieties as Russian) belong exclusively to the Borzoi (*b*).

'Muzzle slightly arched and forehead prominent are typical of the Borzoi, but when the arch is too pronounced or the forehead too prominent, they are faults.

'The skull must be long, oval to the sides, and have a small slip to the back part of the head, finishing by a prominency sharp enough and well pronounced. Every other form is not typical.

'The muzzle is long and thin, and clean, the nostrils rather large and slightly projecting over the lower jaw. The nose must be black (*c*).

'The eye must be full, and of oblong shape (an oblique eye is a defect, and a round one is not typical); it must be of a dark colour in a dark lining (*d*). Its expression is austere, but certainly not when indoors or when the dog is caressed, but at liberty or while hunting.

'The ear is small, thin (its thinness is a proof of high blood), having the form of a wedge. It must be very mobile, and is sometimes carried erect like a horse's ear (*e*).

'This last quality is one of the best proofs of high birth. The hair that covers the ears must be very short, soft as satin, and must not grow in bunches. The dog should carry its neck like an English Greyhound, but the Borzoi's neck is shorter, and is not so straight. The shoulders should be flat and well seen; the elbows must not be turned outwards, but should be clear of the sides of the dog.

'The arch of the back of a dog must be quite regular and make no impression of a hump. The arch seems higher than it really is, because the hind part of the dog is higher than the fore part. The bitch has the back less arched, but even a high arch must not be considered as a great defect.

'The ribs of the Borzoi must descend as low as the elbow. They can be either flat or round, their form depending upon the breadth of the back; but they must never be too round (*f*). The ribs must gradually get smaller to the stomach. The stomach is drawn in and quite hidden behind the groin. The groin of a dog must be small; the less the better. A bitch must have it longer.

'The hindquarters are long and broad. The dog is more sloping than the bitch. A short and drooping loin is a great defect, because it forces the hind legs to be quite straight (*g*).

'The fore legs are quite straight. The bone must be flat from the side, and not round. The foot resembles that of a hare (*h*), with toes of medium length. On each toe grows a bunch of hair, long and thin (*i*). The under part of the paw is of an oblong form.

'The hind legs are parallel one to another, slightly set back (not too much).

'The thighs are flat, with very broad bones. The muscles are flat, long and firm.

'The tail is thin, but strong in its beginning, growing gradually thinner and thinner to the end; it must be elastic, have the form of a sickle, and be of medium length. Its upper part is covered with curly hair, but the hair on the lower part is long and slightly undulated.

'The hair of the dog is curly on the neck, slightly wavy on the back of the dog—as far as the loins—and again more wavy on the thighs, much shorter on the sides, but falls long and satin-like from the chest.

'Personally, we admit as typical colour of the hair only white, grey, yellow and white spotted with grey and yellow (*j*).'

The references shown by letters in parentheses should be read as they add interest to the script.

(*a*) A comparison very popular among Russian hunters.

(*b*) The writer forgets the Greyhounds of Poland, whose tails are exactly of the same shape as the Borzoi, only covered with very short hair.

(*c*) A nose not sufficiently black, even when it has the colour of flesh, must not be considered as proof of bad race. It is simply a symptom of poorness of blood.

(*d*) A light eye and the absence of a dark lining represent the same defect as a light nose.

(*e*) A favourite comparison with Russian amateurs.

(*f*) Not so round as the sides of an English Greyhound.

(*g*) Many huntsmen begin to prefer a sloping loin. The reason is that this form was common to the majority of coursing winners in Russia.

(*h*) Comparison generally used by Russian amateurs. We consider the cat foot a fault for Borzoi.

(*i*) Not for dogs in field condition.

(*j*) All our amateurs were quite astonished when we heard that a black dog (I think its name was 'Argos')* was proclaimed champion in England. This colour is one of the first proofs of a great deal of Crimean or Caucassian blood.

** 'Argos' was, in fact, a black-and-tan, owned by Mr. O. H. Blees, a Russian who was responsible for importing a number of good Borzois into England, some of which were assigned to the Duchess of Newcastle.*

Mrs. J. L. Gibbs' Ch. Galina of Colhugh   *Photo: Gibbs*

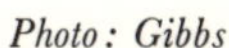

Head Study. Mrs. W. Chadwick's Ch. Winjones Ermolai.

Chapter 3

The Borzoi in America

THE Borzoi was virtually unknown in America before the start of the last decade in the nineteenth century, but in that period a few specimens were imported by Mr. C. Stedman Hanks. These followed the noted 'Elsie' said to have been purchased from Russia by Mr. William Wade of Pennsylvania. A Club for the breed was started in 1904. This was known as the Russian Wolfhound Club, the title name preceding what is now known as the Borzoi Club of America. Type seems to have varied considerably in the early days of the breed and it was not until fresh blood and well typed Borzois were imported from the kennels of the Grand Duke Nicholas that matters began to improve. Up to then, the few Borzoi who had been bred were kept mainly as pets and companions or used to hunt coyotes and other sheep marauders.

Today the breed is well established at all points of the compass in the United States and big specialist shows are common. The American system of defining and classifying their shows is given below, these being extracts from the American Kennel Club's Rules Applying to Registration and Dog Shows, Chapters 4 and 6 respectively. These are reproduced with the kind permission of the A.K.C.

The American Kennel Club's Schedule of Fees is:

Litter Registration, each   5.00
Individual Dog Registration, each   3.00

Change of Ownership, each	2.00
Certified Pedigree—	
Three generations, each	5.00
Four generations, each	10.00
Five generations, each	20.00
The Complete Dog Book	7.00
Pure Bred Dogs—American Kennel Gazette	
—Single Copies	1.00
Subscription Rates—	
One year	8.00
Two years	14.00
Three years	20.00
Canadian and Foreign Postage Extra	
Stud Book Register—	
Single year	2.00
One year	18.00
Foreign Postage Extra	
Duplicate Certificate of Registration	2.00
Duplicate Championship Certificate	3.00
Duplicate Breeders Certificate	2.00
Duplicate C.D., C.D.X., U.D., and T.D.	
Certificates	2.00

Single copies of the *Rules Applying to Registration and Dog Shows, Registration and Field Trial Rules, Beagle Field Trial Rules,* and *Obedience Regulations* are available at no charge on individual request.

The secretary of the parent club of Borzois in America is:

> Mr. Jeff Campbell,
> Borzoi Club of America,
> P.O. Box 28,
> Mt. Victoria, Md. 20661.

and he will be glad to send information of the club's activities, also name and addresses of the secretaries of regional clubs and associations in the U.S.A.

Dog Shows Defined

Section 1. A member show is a show at which championship points may be awarded, given by a club or association which is a member of the American Kennel Club.

Section 2. A licensed show is a show at which championship points may be awarded, given by a club or association which is not a member of the American Kennel Club but which has been specially licensed by the American Kennel Club to give the specific show designated in the licence.

Section 3. A member or licensed all-breed club may apply to the American Kennel Club for approval to hold a show at which championship points may be awarded with entries restricted to puppies that are eligible for entry in the regular puppy class and dogs that have been placed first, second or third in a regular class at a show at which championship points were awarded, provided the club submitting such an application has held at least one show annually for at least ten years immediately prior to the year in which application for a show so restricted is made, and further provided that there shall not have been less than 900 dogs entered in its show (or in one of its shows if the club holds more than one show a year) in the year preceding the year in which application is made for its first show with entries so restricted.

When an application for this type of restricted entry show has been approved by the American Kennel Club the only dogs eligible for entry shall be puppies that are eligible for entry in the regular puppy class and those dogs that have been placed first, second or third in a regular class at a show at which championship points were awarded held not less than sixty days prior to the first day of the show at which entries will be so restricted.

However, a club making application to hold a show restricted to entries of dogs as specified above may further restrict entries by excluding all puppies or all puppies six months and under nine months and/or by excluding dogs that have placed third or dogs that have placed second and third, provided the extent of these further restrictions are specified on the application.

Any club whose application has been approved to hold a show with restricted entries as described in this section shall indicate the extent of the restrictions in its premium list.

Section 4. A member or licensed all-breed club may apply to the American Kennel Club for approval to hold a show at which championship points may be awarded with entries restricted to dogs that are champions on the records of The American Kennel Club and dogs that have been credited with one or more championship points, provided the club submitting such an application has held at least one show annually for at least fifteen years immediately prior to the year in which application for a show so restricted is made, and further provided that there shall not have been less than 1200 dogs entered in its show (or in one of its shows if the club holds more than one show a year) in the year preceding the year in which application is made for its first show with entries so restricted.

When an application for this type of restricted entry show has been approved by the American Kennel Club, the only dogs eligible for entry shall be those dogs that have been recorded as champions and dogs that have been credited with one or more championship points as a result of competition at shows held not less than sixty days prior to the first day of the show at which entries will be so restricted.

However, a club making application to hold a show restricted to entries of dogs as specified above, may further restrict entries by excluding all puppies or all puppies six months and under nine months and/or by excluding dogs that have not been credited with at least one major championship point rating, provided the extent of these further restrictions are specified on the application.

Any club whose application has been approved to hold a show with restricted entries as described in this section shall indicate the extent of the restrictions in its premium list.

Section 5. A member or licensed show with a limited entry, at which championship points may be awarded may be given by a club or association in the event said club or association considers it necessary to *Limit* the *Total Entry* at its show due to the limitations of space. The total number of entries to be accepted together with the reason therefore, must be indicated on the cover or title page of the *Premium List*. A specified closing date, in accordance with Chapter 9, Section 9, must be indicated in the premium list together with a statement that entries will close on said date or when the limit has been reached, if prior thereto. No entries can be accepted, cancelled or substituted after the entry is closed. The specified closing date shall be used in determining whether a dog is eligible for the Novice Classes at the show.

Section 6. A speciality show is a show given by a club or association formed for the improvement of any one breed of pure-bred dogs, at which championship points may be awarded to said breed.

Section 7. An American-bred speciality show is a show for American-bred dogs only, given by a member club or association formed for the improvement of any one breed of pure-breed dogs at which championship points may be awarded to said breed.

Section 8. A sanctioned match is an informal meeting at which pure-bred dogs may compete but not for championship points, held by a club or association whether or not a member of the American Kennel Club by obtaining the sanction of the American Kennel Club.

Dog Show Classifications

Section 1. The following breeds and/or varieties of breeds, divided by groups, shall be all the breeds and/or varieties of breeds for which regular classes of the American Kennel Club may be provided at any show held under American Kennel Club rules. The Board of Directors may either add to, transfer from one group to another, or delete from said list of breeds, and/or varieties of breeds, whenever in its opinion registrations of such breed and/or variety of breed in the Stud Book justify such action.

GROUP 1—SPORTING DOGS

Pointers
Pointers (German Short-haired)
Pointers (German Wire-haired)
Retrievers (Chesapeake Bay)
Retrievers (Curly-coated)
Retrievers (Flat-coated)
Retrievers (Golden)
Retrievers (Labrador)
Setters (English)
Setters (Gordon)
Setters (Irish)
Spaniels (American Water)
Spaniels (Brittany)
Spaniels (Clumber)
Spaniels (Cocker)
  Three varieties: Solid color, black. Solid color, other than black, including black and tan. Parti-color.
Spaniels (English Cocker)
Spaniels (English Springer)
Spaniels (Field)
Spaniels (Irish Water)
Spaniels (Sussex)
Spaniels (Welsh Springer)
Vizslas
Weimaraners
Wire-haired Pointing Griffons

GROUP 2—HOUNDS

Afghan Hounds
Basenjis
Basset Hounds
Beagles
  Two varieties: Not exceeding 13 inches in height. Over 13 inches but not exceeding 15 inches in height.
Black and Tan Coonhounds
Bloodhounds
Borzois
Dachshunds
  Three varieties: Long-haired. Smooth. Wire-haired.
Foxhounds (American)
Foxhounds (English)
Greyhounds

Harriers
Irish Wolfhounds
Norwegian Elkhounds
Otter Hounds
Rhodesian Ridgebacks
Salukis
Scottish Deerhounds
Whippets

GROUP 3—WORKING DOGS

Alaskan Malamutes
Belgian Malinois
Belgian Sheepdogs
Belgian Tervuren
Bernese Mountain Dogs
Bouviers des Flandres
Boxers
Briards
Bullmastiffs
Collies
    Two varieties: Rough. Smooth.
Doberman Pinschers
German Shepherd Dogs
Giant Schnauzers
Great Danes
Great Pyrenees
Komondorok
Kuvaszok
Mastiffs
Newfoundlands
Old English Sheepdogs
Pulik
Rottweilers
St. Bernards
Samoyeds
Shetland Sheepdogs
Siberian Huskies
Standard Schnauzers
Welsh Corgis (Cardigan)
Welsh Corgis (Pembroke)

Mrs. J. Bennett-Heard's Ch. Keepers the Baron

GROUP 4—TERRIERS

Airedale Terriers
American Staffordshire Terriers
Australian Terriers
Bedlington Terriers
Border Terriers
Bull Terriers

Two varieties: White. Coloured.
Cairn Terriers
Dandie Dinmont Terriers
Fox Terriers
   Two varieties: Smooth. Wire.
Irish Terriers
Kerry Blue Terriers
Lakeland Terriers
Manchester Terriers
   Two varieties: Standard, over 12 pounds and not exceeding
      22 pounds. Toy (in Toy Group).
Miniature Schnauzers
Norwich Terriers
Scottish Terriers
Sealyham Terriers
Skye Terriers
Welsh Terriers
West Highland White Terriers

Mrs. A. Thornwell's Ch. Wellthornes Kalinka

GROUP 5—TOYS

Affenpinschers
Brussels Griffons
Chihuahuas
   Two varieties: Smooth coat. Long coat.
English Toy Spaniels
   Two varieties: King Charles and Ruby. Blenheim and Prince
      Charles.
Italian Greyhounds
Japanese Spaniels
Maltese
Manchester Terriers
   Two varieties: Toy, not exceeding 12 pounds. Standard (in
      Terrier Group).
Miniature Pinschers
Papillons
Pekingese
Pomeranians
Poodles
   Three varieties: Toy, not exceeding 10 inches. Miniature (in
      Non-Sporting Group). Standard (in Non-Sporting
      Group).
Pugs
Shih Tzu
Silky Terriers
Yorkshire Terriers

GROUP 6—NON-SPORTING DOGS

Boston Terriers

Bulldogs
Chow Chows
Dalmatians
French Bulldogs
Keeshonden
Lhasa Apsos
Poodles
    Three varieties: Miniature, over 10 inches and not exceeding
      15 inches. Standard, over 15 inches. Toy (in Toy Group).
Schipperkes

Section 2. No class shall be provided for any dog under six months of age except at sanctioned matches when approved by the American Kennel Club.

Section 3. The regular classes of the American Kennel Club shall be as follows:
Puppy
Novice
Bred-by-Exhibitor
American-bred
Open
Winners

Section 4. The Puppy Class shall be for dogs that are six months of age and over, but under twelve months, that were whelped in the United States of America or Canada, and that are not champions. The age of a dog shall be calculated up to and inclusive of the first day of a show. For example, a dog whelped on 1st January is eligible to compete in a puppy class as at show the first day of which is 1st July of the same year and may continue to compete in puppy classes at shows up to and including a show the first day of which is the 31st day of December of the same year, but is not eligible to compete in a puppy class at a show the first day of which is 1st January of the following year.

Section 5. The Novice Class shall be for dogs six months of age and over, whelped in the United States of America or Canada, which have not, prior to the date of closing of entries, won three first prizes in the Novice Class, a first prize in Bred-by-Exhibitor, American-bred, or Open Classes, nor one or more points toward their championships.

Section 6. The Bred-by-Exhibitor Class shall be for dogs whelped in the United States of America, or, if individually registered in the American Kennel Club Stud Book, for dogs whelped in Canada, that are six months of age and over, that are not champions, and that are owned wholly or in part by the person or by the spouse of the person who was the breeder or one of the breeders of record.

    Dogs entered in this class must be handled in the class by

an owner or by a member of the immediate family of an owner.

For purposes of this section, the members of an immediate family are: husband, wife, father, mother, son, daughter, brother, sister.

Section 7. The American-bred Class shall be for all dogs (except champions) six months of age and over, whelped in the United States of America, by reason of a mating which took place in the United States of America.

Section 8. The Open Class shall be for any dog six months. of age or over except in a member speciality club show held only for American-bred dogs, in which case the Open Class shall be only for American-bred dogs.

Section 9. The Winners Class, at shows in which the American bred and Open Classes are divided by sex, also shall be divided by sex and each division shall be open only to undefeated dogs of the same sex which have won first prizes in either the Puppy, Novice, Bred-by-Exhibitor, American-bred or Open Classes, excepting only in the event that where either the Puppy, Novice or Bred-by-Exhibitor Class shall not have been divided by sex, dogs of the same sex winning second or third prizes but not having been defeated by a dog of the same sex may compete in the Winners Class provided for their sex. At shows where the American-bred and Open Classes are not divided by sex there shall be but one Winners Class which shall be open only to undefeated dogs of either sex which have won first prizes in either the Puppy, Novice, Bred-by-Exhibitor, American-bred or Open Classes. There shall be no entry fee for competition in the Winners Class.

After the winners' prize has been awarded in one of the sex divisions, where the Winners Class has been divided by sex, any second or third prize winning dog otherwise undefeated in its sex, which however, has been beaten in its class by the dog awarded winners, shall compete with the other eligible dogs for Reserve Winners. After the Winners prize has been awarded, where the Winners Class is not divided by sex, any otherwise undefeated dog which has been placed second in any previous class to the dog awarded winner shall compete with the remaining first prize winners, for reserve winner. No eligible dog may be withheld from competition.

Winners Classes shall be allowed only at shows where American-bred and Open Classes shall be given.

A member speciality club holding a show for American-bred dogs only may include Winners Classes, provided the necessary regular classes are included in the classification.

A member club holding a show with restricted entries may include Winners Classes provided the necessary regular classes are included in the classification.

Section 10. No Winners Class, or any class resembling it, shall be given at sanctioned matches.

Section 11. Bench show committees may provide such other classes of recognized breeds or recognized varieties of breeds as they may choose, provided they do not conflict with the conditions of the above mentioned classes and are judged before Best of Breed competition.

Local classes, however, may not be divided by sex in shows at which local group classes are provided.

No class may be given in which more than one breed or recognized variety of breed may be entered, except as provided in these rules and regulations.

Section 12. A club that provides Winners Classes shall also provide competition for Best of Breed or for Best of Variety in those breeds for which varieties are provided in this chapter. The awards in this competition shall be Best of Breed or Best of Variety of Breed.

The following categories of dogs may be entered and shown in this competition:

Dogs that are Champions of Record.

Dogs which according to their owners' records have completed the requirements for a championship but whose championships are unconfirmed. The showing of dogs whose championships are unconfirmed is limited to a period of ninety days from the date of the show where a dog completed the requirements for a championship according to the owners' records.

In addition, the Winners dog and Winners bitch (or the dog awarded winner, if only one winner's prize has been awarded). together with any undefeated dogs that have competed at the show only in additional non-regular classes shall compete for Best of Breed or Best of Variety of Breed.

If the Winners dog or Winners bitch is awarded Best of Breed or Best of Variety of Breed, it shall be automatically awarded Best of Winners; otherwise, the winners' dog and winners' bitch shall be judged together for Best of Winners following the judging of Best of Breed or Best of Variety of Breed. The dog designated Best of Winners shall be entitled to the number of points based on the number of dogs or bitches competing in the regular classes, whichever is greater. In the event that winner is awarded in only one sex, there shall be no Best of Winners award.

After Best of Breed or Best of Variety of Breed and Best of Winners have been awarded, the judge shall select Best of Opposite Sex to Best of Breed or Best of Variety of Breed. Eligible for this award are:

Dogs of the opposite sex to Best of Breed or Best of Variety of Breed that have been entered for Best of Breed competition.

The dog awarded winner of the opposite sex to the Best of Breed or Best of Variety of Breed.

Any undefeated dogs of the opposite sex to Best of Breed or Best of Variety of Breed which have competed at the show only in additional non-regular classes.

Section 13. At speciality shows for breeds in which there are varieties as specified in Chapter 6, Section 1, and which are held apart from all-breed shows, Best of Breed shall be judged following the judging of Best of each variety and best of opposite sex to best of each variety. Best of Opposite Sex to Best of Breed shall also be judged. Dogs eligible for Best of Opposite Sex to Best-of-Breed competition will be found among the bests of variety or the bests of opposite sex to bests of variety, according to the sex of the dog placed Best of Breed.

At an all-breed show (even if a speciality club shall designate classes as its speciality show), the judge of a breed in which there are show varieties shall make no placings beyond Best of Variety and Best of Opposite Sex to Best of Variety.

Section 14. A club or association holding a show may give six group classes not divided by sex, such groups to be arranged in same order and to comprise the same breeds and recognized varieties of breeds as hereinbefore set forth in Chapter 2 and Section 1 of Chapter 6. All dogs designated by their respective breed judges Best of Breed at the show at which these group classes shall be given shall be eligible to compete in the group classes to which they belong according to this grouping, and all dogs designated Best of Variety in those breeds with more than one recognized variety, shall be eligible to compete in the group classes to which they belong according to this grouping. All entries for these group classes shall be made after judging of the regular classes of the American Kennel Club has been finished and no entry fee shall be charged. In the event that the owner of a dog designated Best of Breed or Best of Variety shall not exhibit the dog in the group class to which it is eligible, no other dog of the same breed or variety of breed shall be allowed to compete.

Section 15. A club giving group classes must also give a Best in Show, the winner to be entitled 'Best Dog in Show'. No entry fee shall be charged but the six group winners must compete.

Section 16. A club or association holding a show, if it gives brace classes in the several breeds and recognized varieties of breeds, may also give six brace group classes, not divided by sex; such groups to be arranged in the same order and to comprise the same breeds and recognized varieties of breeds as hereinbefore set forth in Chapter 2 and Section 1 of Chapter 6. All braces of dogs designated by their respective breed judges as Best of Breed or Best of Variety as the case may be at shows

Mrs. J. Bennett-Heard's Ch. Keepers Michael-Angelo

at which these brace group classes shall be given, shall be eligible to compete in the brace group classes to which they belong according to this grouping. All entries for these brace group classes shall be made after the judging of the regular classes of the American Kennel Club has been finished and no entry fee shall be charged. In the event that the owner of a brace of dogs designated Best of Breed or Best of Variety shall not exhibit the brace of dogs in the group class to which it is eligible, no other brace of dogs of the same breed or variety of breed shall be allowed to compete.

Section 17. If a club or association holding a show shall give these six group classes, it must also give a 'Best Brace in Show' in which the six braces of dogs winning the first prizes in the six group classes must compete, but for which no entry fee shall be charged. The winner shall be entitled 'The Best Brace in Show'.

Section 18. A club or association holding a show, if it gives team classes in the several breeds and recognized varieties of breeds, may also give six team group classes not divided by sex, such groups to be arranged in the same order and to comprise the same breeds and recognized varieties of breeds as hereinbefore set forth in Chapter 2 and Section 1 of Chapter 6. All teams of dogs designated by their respective breed judges as Best of Breed or Best of Variety as the case may be at shows at which these team group classes shall be given, shall be eligible to compete in the team group classes to which they belong according to this grouping. All entries for these team group classes shall be made after the judging of the regular classes of the American Kennel Club has been finished and no entry fee shall be charged. In the event that the owners of a team of dogs designated Best of Breed or Best of Variety shall not exhibit the team of dogs in the group class to which it is eligible, no other team of dogs of the same breed or variety of breed shall be allowed to compete.

Section 19. If a club or association holding a show shall give these six group classes it must also give a 'Best Team in Show' in which the six teams of dogs winning the first prizes in the six group classes must compete, but for which no entry fee shall be charged. The winner shall be entitled 'The Best Team in Show'.

Section 20. A club or association holding a show may give six group classes not divided by sex, open only to local dogs (as designated in its premium list), such groups to be arranged in the same order and to comprise the same breeds and recognized varieties of breeds as hereinbefore set forth in Chatper 2 and Section 1 of Chapter 6. All dogs designated by their respective breed judges 'Best in Local Class of the Breed' or 'Best in Local Class of the Variety of Breed' at the show at which these group classes shall be given shall be eligible to compete in the group classes to which they belong according to this grouping. No entry fee shall be charged. In the event that the owner of the dog designated 'Best in Local Class' shall not exhibit the dog in the group class to which it is eligible, no other dog of the same breed or variety of breed shall be allowed to compete.

Section 21. A club giving local group classes may also give a 'Best Local Dog in Show'. No entry fee shall be charged but the local group winners must compete.

Section 22. A club or association holding a show may offer Junior Showmanship competition if it so chooses.

The classes and procedure shall conform to the American Kennel Club regulations governing Junior Showmanship as adopted by the Board of Directors.

Section 23. The Miscellaneous Class shall be for pure-bred dogs of such breeds as may be designated by the Board of Directors of the American Kennel Club. No dog shall be eligible for entry in the Miscellaneous Class unless the owner has been granted an Indefinite Listing Privilege, and unless the I.L.P. number is given on the entry form. Application for an Indefinite Listing Privilege shall be made on a form provided by the A.K.C. and when submitted must be accompanied by a fee set by the Board of Directors.

All Miscellaneous Breeds shall be shown together in a single class except that the class may be divided by sex if so specified in the premium list. There shall be no further competition for dogs entered in this class.

The ribbons for first, second, third and fourth prizes in this class shall be rose, brown, light green, and grey, respectively.

At present the Miscellaneous Class is open to the following breeds:

Akitas	Ibizan Hounds
Australian Cattle Dogs	Miniature Bull Terriers
Australian Kelpies	Soft-Coated Wheaten Terriers
Bichon Frise	Spinoni Italiani
Border Collies	Staffordshire Bull Terriers
Cavalier King Charles	Tibetan Terriers
Spaniels	

Section 24. A registered dog that is six months of age or over and of a breed for which a classification is offered in the premium list may be entered in a show for Exhibition Only at the regular entry fee provided the dog has been awarded first prize in one of the regular classes at a licensed or member show held prior to the closing of entries of the show in which the Exhibition Only entry is made, and provided further that the premium list has not specified that entries for Exhibition Only will not be accepted. The name and date of the show at which the dog was awarded the first prize must be stated on the entry form.

A dog entered for Exhibition Only shall not be shown in any class or competition at that show.

The American Standard for Borzois

The American Standard for Borzois was revised in 1972 this being approved by the American Kennel Club on 13th June of the same year. It varies appreciably in its wording with the English version while offering more detail in its description of the perfect Borzoi. It is reproduced below by kind permission of the A.K.C.

REVISED STANDARD FOR BORZOIS

The Board of Directors of the American Kennel Club has approved the following revised Standard for Borzois submitted by the Borzoi Club of America.

General Appearance: The Borzoi was originally bred for the coursing of wild game on more or less open terrain, relying on sight rather than scent. To accomplish this purpose, the Borzoi needed particular structural qualities to chase, catch and hold his quarry. Special emphasis is placed on sound running gear, strong neck and jaws, courage and agility, combined with proper condition. The Borzoi should always possess unmistakable elegance, with flowing lines, graceful in motion or repose. Males, masculine without coarseness; bitches, feminine and refined.

Head: Skull slightly domed, long and narrow, with scarcely any perceptible stop, inclined to be Roman-nosed. Jaws long, powerful and deep, somewhat finer in bitches but not snipy. Teeth strong and clean with either an even or a scissors bite. Missing teeth should be penalized. Nose large and black.

Ears: Small and fine in quality, lying back on the neck when in repose with the tips when thrown back almost touching behind occiput; raised when at attention.

Eyes: Set somewhat obliquely, dark in colour, intelligent but rather soft in expression; never round, full nor staring, nor light in colour; eye rims dark; inner corner midway between tip of nose and occiput.

Neck: Clean, free from throatiness; slightly arched, very powerful and well set on.

Shoulders: Sloping, fine at the withers and free from coarseness or lumber.

Chest: Rather narrow, with great depth of brisket.

Ribs: Only slightly sprung, but very deep, giving room for heart and lung play.

Back: Rising a little at the loins in a graceful curve.

Loins: Extremely muscular, but rather tucked up, owing to the great depth of chest and comparative shortness of back and ribs.

Forelegs: Bones straight and somewhat flattened like blades, with the narrower edge forward. The elbows have free play and are turned neither in nor out. Pasterns strong.

Feet: Hare-shaped, with well-arched knuckles, toes close and well padded.

Hindquarters: Long, very muscular and powerful with well-bent stifles; somewhat wider than the forequarters; strong first and second thighs; hocks clean and well let down; legs parallel when viewed from the rear.

Dewclaws: Dewclaws, if any, on the hind legs are generally removed; dewclaws on the forelegs may be removed.

Tail: Long, set on and carried low in a graceful curve.

Coat: Long, silky (not woolly), either flat, wavy or rather curly. On the head, ears and front of legs it should be short and smooth; on the neck the frill should be profuse and rather curly. Feather on hindquarters and tail, long and profuse, less so on chest and back of forelegs.

Colour: Any colour or combination of colours is acceptable.

Size: Mature males should be at least 28 inches at the withers and mature bitches at least 26 inches at the withers. Dogs and bitches below these respective limits should be severely penalized; dogs and bitches above the respective limits should not be penalized as long as extra size is not acquired at the expense of symmetry, speed, and staying quality. Range in weight for males from 75 to 105 pounds and for bitches from 15 to 20 pounds less.

Gait: Front legs must reach well out in front with pasterns strong and springy. Hackneyed motion with mincing gait is not desired nor is weaving and crossing. However, while the hind legs are wider apart than the front, the feet tend to move closer to the centre line when the dog moves at a fast trot. When viewed from the side there should be noticeable drive with a ground-covering stride from well-angulated stifles and hocks. The over-all appearance in motion should be that of effortless power, endurance, speed, agility, smoothness and grace.

Faults: The foregoing description is that of the ideal Borzoi. Any deviation from the above described dog must be penalized to the extent of the deviation, keeping in mind the importance of the contribution of the various features towards the basic original purpose of the breed.

Mrs. L. Pearson's and Mr. K. L. Prior's
Ch. Zomahli Gratseeya

Mrs. J. L. Gibbs' Winjones Riskay

Photo: Gibbs

Eileen Garrett with some of the Borzoi which
appeared in the film 'War and Peace'   *B.B.C.*

Chapter 4

Breeding

MOST people owning a handsome Borzoi will be tempted at some
time or other to try their hand at reproducing his or her kind.
The breed is one which excites tremendous admiration in
public. Yet in these enlightened times, as far as dogs are concerned, few folk recognize the breed and even told its name will
know how to spell it! Nevertheless, it is a breed which many
people will be glad to 'know' about and acquire for themselves,
so the sales potential is high.

A breeder's aim is to produce a Borzoi which is at least as
good as the one he owns, better if possible. If he can achieve the
latter then he will have done a worthwhile service to his breed
and obtain for himself a real sense of achievement. Unfortunately, few breeders possess what can be claimed as a sound
working knowledge of genetics, but oddly enough many dog
lovers do have what can be termed as 'an eye' for a dog. This
instinct has held many in good stead in their careers and
enabled them to produce by good assessment of mating pairs,
some worthwhile stock.

Look first of all at your bitch. Is she good?—has she turned
out as well as you expected? What have the experts said about
her? Has she a good pedigree, a good strain? If you are a lucky
owner then you can answer 'yes' to most of these questions and
feel heartened at least in the thought that having picked the
right dog for her, you stand a fairly good chance of breeding
something nice from her. If she is just an average specimen with

a fair share of faults and not from the pre-eminent bloodline in her breed then your task is perhaps more difficult, but at least you have the right to try and improve upon her by careful selection of her mate. Providing you have a reasonably good bitch who is sound both physically and temperamentally, never be persuaded to delay your hand at breeding. Too many people with a flair for breeding good dogs have been kept in the background by others in the fancy who have told them not to breed because their bitch 'was not good enough'. An *average* bitch with type is good enough to breed from, providing you intend to improve upon her. The only ones to keep free from puppies are the vicious and unsound. Bad mothers too are a nuisance, but one can seldom find out their shortcomings without giving them a litter first, although sometimes this vicissitude runs in families of bitches, which at least will forewarn you and allow you to take precautionary measures to protect the puppies and your interests.

Mrs. J. L. Gibbs' Opal of Fortrouge
Photo: Gibbs

If you plan to breed Borzois regularly, as opposed to the single venture with just one pet bitch, then it is important to steel yourself to the tenet of keeping only good bitches in your kennel. You will find as you progress that some dogs will become no more than 'passengers' to the kennel. This does not refer to the old and much-loved animal who has been in the home for many years and is part and parcel of the family. A pal of this kind deserves and indeed should have every care and comfort you can bestow upon it. My comment refers to the *passé* breeding stock which sometimes accumulates in the kennel, serving no useful purpose and merely making expense. You can serve such an animal better by finding it a good home somewhere. There it will receive individual attention (which you may well be unable to give it) and become a pet in its own right with a nice family. Much better for it this way than to let it finish its days in a kennel, just enjoying human companionship for very brief periods.

The Pedigree

To many this is a mere piece of paper. They take it home when they buy their dog, put it in a safe place somewhere and promptly forget about it. To you as a breeder however, it is an important document. Remember though that a dog is only as good as its pedigree and no matter how superb and handsome she is to look at, if a bitch has in her blood some poor ancestry this will fashion the shape and quality of her stock issue. Conversely, no pedigree is worth any more than the dog it refers to. You might have a pedigree before you brimful of champions—the best in the breed. It means very little if your Borzoi is a poor specimen! The ideal situation is to own a good-looking dog with a good-looking pedigree. From such a dog or bitch you stand then a very reasonable chance of producing good puppies. It is important now to study your bitch's pedigree. What has she behind her? Do her ancestors boast the prestige of a noted strain or are they mediocre in form and lacking note? Try and obtain the help of a person well steeped in Borzoi lore and modern breed history. He or she should know the dogs of the past twenty years, will probably have judged most of them or at least watched them being judged from the ringside. He will recollect their stamp, remember their careers, their colours, size and reputations, no doubt.

He will remember their faults too. It is odd how experts, even the unbiased ones will recall faults easier than good points. But you will want to know both and you must press for information on the dogs whose names appear on the piece of paper before you. If one man cannot supply enough ask others, but refer only to people with good reputations themselves—people who

can impart facts which are authentic, not mere guesswork or
hearsay. Draft out your pedigree on a large piece of paper
and beneath the name of every dog and bitch ancestor in its own
square write in the data you have gleaned. Try and get details
on *every* animal, even if it means writing to people long since out
of the breed. You will often find someone in their family who
recalls the dog their sister or brother owned and can tell you
something useful about it. But do not forget to enclose a stamped
addressed envelope. From the facts you accumulate you should
be able to form a perfect word picture of the ancestral qualities
and faults behind your bitch, probably sufficient to ensure that
when you come to select a stud dog for her you will at least be
forearmed with knowledge which will enable you to avoid in
her puppies any duplication of her faults capable of being passed
on in double measure to her progeny.

Pedigrees can usually be relied upon these days. In the very
old days of all breeds and Borzois would be no exception, records
of a dog's breeding would have been kept casually, to say the
least. In certain cases, such information was jealously guarded
by owners and breeders, especially if the specimens involved
were good ones. The pedigree would then be thought more a
'secret formula' which provided a good specimen, than what
we know it as, viz: a breeding record to be used freely in an
effort to improve subsequent generations.

Mrs. J. L. Gibbs' Opal of Fortrouge and
Mrs. N. Sanderson's Sholwood Silvermere
Photo: Gibbs

Breeding Methods

Line-Breeding

This is the most popular system of breeding dogs today. It is quite simple, providing care is taken not to introduce stock which falls below standard quality. Line-breeding is really the mating of relatives and entails the following crosses:

> Grandson to Granddam
> Grandsire to Grand-daughter
> Cousin to Cousin

and includes the mating of aunts and nephews, uncles and nieces and half-brothers to sisters. Briefly, it means that quite closely related animals can be mated, but *not* immediate relatives such as brother and sister which form of union falls into the category of in-breeding, discussed next. In line-breeding, whereas the pedigrees of both mates should carry similar blood-lines, it is not essential that they have all the same blood-lines and a common ancestor may well appear twice in the last five generations. When assessing the pedigrees of both the dam and her prospective mate, as you will do in due course, it is often a good thing if you can detect one or two strong, vital lines to a dominant sire or dam whose type and quality you wish to aim for in the litter to be bred. Having found this, it is sometimes a good thing if the remaining parts of the pedigrees are not involved with effective blood-lines capable of counteracting, perhaps adversely, the effect of ancestral sire or dam on whose type and characteristics you have set your sights. The method of line-breeding is a sound one, although you may well have to wait patiently for results, unlike in-breeding which while faster is fraught with greater dangers. Line-breeding takes a time to establish purity of strain and once this point has been reached, not a lot can be done to improve further while your own kennel stock is being employed in the programme of breeding. Then you will have to consider the introduction of fresh blood and while such a move has its hazards, with care you can maintain the purity you have achieved in your strain and inject it with a new lease of life.

In-Breeding

This is the mating of closely related dogs, i.e. son to mother, father to daughter, brother to sister. It should be done only in lines which are very strong, showing a high standard of type, health, soundness and temperament. That these characteristics need to be perpetuated with each and every generation goes without saying and in-breeding will aid such dominance. Only really first-class material must be employed and if you try in-breeding with lowly stock you will do no more than quickly 'fix' lowly points in your strain. This is the idea of in-breeding—it is to secure firmly the *good* points in your strain, but if your strain is liberally endowed with a number of indifferent features, then it will establish some of these for you too! That is why only animals which fall into a category which can claim freedom from *distinct* defects can be permitted entry to such a breeding programme. Rigorous culling of unwanted stock must take place prior to the planned furtherance of each generation. The breeder must be honest with himself, recognize where weaknesses exist in his stock and only employ parental pairs which he knows in his heart can maintain the high standard of his kennel. If he omits this assessment he is doomed to failure for the longer defects are permitted to exist the more time and effort will be needed to eradicate them, always with the very real possibility of degeneration creeping in to ruin the work of years.

Out-crossing

In serious dog-breeding, the out-cross is today seldom employed. The system has its value when the out-cross employed is a dog which has some connection with the original strain, linked perhaps through a pre-potent line. In the old days, an out-cross was used to improve a deficiency which it was felt existed in a working strain. For example, a Bulldog was put to Greyhounds by Lord Oxford because it was felt the latter breed needed stamina. Whether such a move proved worthwhile we do not know, but the only out-cross system of any value is when an outside dog can improve the health and type of a strain which has deteriorated, perhaps due to slapdash breeding. Some folk believe that an out-cross dog can improve, invigorate, even produce big winners from a negative strain. This is not so and if by chance such a big winner did arise from the strain it would be no more than a 'sport', which is a good specimen, but without anything worthwhile in its blood and probably incapable of passing on even mediocre qualities in his issue.

If an out-cross must be employed and very often in far-flung districts where members of the breed are really sparse and the bitch owner has little or no choice, this can occur, then at least make sure that both parents-to-be are sound and healthy in all departments before allowing any union. If however, an out-cross is planned with a specific purpose in mind then make sure that the dog has factors which render him at least competent to correct any in-bred faults which the bitch possesses. It must be remembered that a sire endowed with such factors and able to rectify the fault is a much better agent as an out-cross than a dog with such strong and dominant blood-lines that he can

Mrs. E. E. Garrett's Edgelmclere Hiawatha
Photo: Youel

Mrs. L. Pearson's and Mr. K. L. Prior's
Ch. Zomahli Gueroy

completely submerge the fault, yet cause to arise to the surface some bad feature, never suspected. The breeder must be prepared in his out-cross results for an uneven litter and perhaps experience some disappointment at the apparent lack of success of the exercise. Very often the good points expected will appear in the second generation, the grandchildren, rather than the initial progeny.

The Bitch

You have now to decide whether your own bitch (assuming you have one) is to be employed in your breeding programme or whether you intend to buy one. Many people believe that the female is the more important of a mating pair, at least as far as determining the quality of her puppies is concerned. It is an acknowledged fact that whereas it is easier to assess a dog's abilities at stud by virtue of the greater number of offspring he produces, a bitch's progeny must necessarily be much fewer. Consider objectively therefore, the female lines as far as ever possible because tail-female (which is the dam's dam's dam—or family) is more important than tail-male (which is the sire's sire's sire—or line).

This means that you *must* have a good bitch if you are to breed really *good* puppies. It has been pointed out in earlier pages that you are entitled to use any sound, healthy and reasonably typical bitch for breeding in a fair effort to improve on her particular virtues through the medium of her puppies. However, if show stock is your intent, then you will need to aim a little higher than a mediocre bitch as your producer. Obviously, with a good bitch you might breed some very good puppies with quite an ordinary stud dog, but even a successful sire may well fail to produce anything but ordinary stock from a plain bitch.

You should buy the best bitch you can afford. Now, this does not mean a bitch has to be expensive, but if you get the opportunity to purchase a young female of obvious worth at a fair price she may well repay you twenty-fold. Seek an adult bitch of not more than twenty months or a well grown puppy as free from faults in her type and construction as possible. Always employ either a knowledgeable companion to advise you or put your trust in a reputable Borzoi kennel of which there are a good number. Make sure you know the breed Standard before you start negotiating and put in a lot of time at major shows (especially championship events) where the breed is on display and being judged. Listen to the competent authorities talk about the exhibits and the judging results. See whether you can follow their lines of thought for yourself. Make sure that the people you listen to know what they are talking about. Too many folk in dogs 'think' they know. Many years experience in a breed such as the Borzoi qualifies *most* people to pontificate reliably on the dog, but length of time in the breed does not necessarily make an expert. Some enthusiasts can learn in five years what it takes others thirty years to assimilate. As in life, some do better and learn quicker at things than do their colleagues. The person who really knows is usually a well-established person in Borzois, either a noted breeder, judge or writer. Seek out such a figurehead and learn from him or her. However, never expect to come by the information you want too easily, certainly never take it without proffering thanks for it. It has probably taken your informant many years to come by, acquired over periods of stress and bitter disappointments and this should be borne in mind.

Knowing now something of the breed you will commence your search. Have nothing to do with the bitch who is too small, shelly and fine. Such a female is not equipped for the rigours of puppy breeding, quite apart from being untypical in appearance. A good Borzoi bitch must have some substance plenty of room inside and an adequate width of pelvis. It is important, too, that she be quite feminine—a doggy bitch is objectionable. Check her teeth to ensure that she has a good level mouth and the dental condition is good, as is that of the gums. Watch for signs of nervousness, but bear in mind that many young females are ill-at-ease in the company of strangers and what might seem nervousness is no more than acute suspicion of your presence. The matter should be followed up for your own satisfaction however, just as you should do with any other feature of your intended purchase which worries you. Take each 'worry' as it comes, eliminating them one by one, not only by judicious questioning but by actual physical handling of the subject until you are completely satisfied.

Ensure that the bitch is amply boned and carries great depth of rib and brisket. Looked at sideways, the depth should reach *at least* to a line passing through the point of elbow. The great arch of back in a Borzoi carries tremendous importance; it being essential to the speed and versatility of action this breed is noted for. Check her shoulders closely; their emplacement should be such that the scapula is well laid back thereby allowing good fore-action and providing for elegance and balance of the body's general structure. The hindquarters are made to propel the dog and the loins in particular need to be very powerful, the second thigh requiring good development and the stifle well bent with hocks let down nicely. Like the forelegs which need to be strong and straight to support the body weight in front, the hind limbs must be straight and clean too and the pasterns firm without any slackness.

The bitch *must* have a typical good Borzoi head. Heads are

Mrs. L. Pearson's and Mr. K. L. Prior's
Ch. Zomahli Igrock

important in all breeds, but nevertheless a good brood bitch has to be chosen for *overall* virtues and no one feature should particularly outshine the others, especially to the point of exaggeration, which is a fault in itself! The head should be of great length and the jaw very strongly made. Snipiness, i.e. a shallow and pointed weak muzzle is a bad fault. Femininity is of absolute importance and coarseness and dogginess are characteristics to be despised in a bitch. Look at her eyes, although if her expression is true, it is reasonable to have at least some confidence that the eyes are right. However, they must be dark—light eyes suggest shrewdness rather than intelligence and impart a somewhat alien expression. The shape of the correct Borzoi eye is almond and the rim being dark. Round eyes give a staring, vapid outlook which is quite wrong. The emplacement of the eyes should be well back and set in obliquely. Deviation from any one of these required features will mar a Borzoi's true expression.

In the matter of colour, it is wise perhaps to select a bitch with conventional coat, dark hounds being attractive to some, but not conducive to the production of facile selling progeny. Coat itself has importance in that a bitch with a 'naturally' poor coat will never prove a useful brood. Allowing for time of the year and the fact that a Borzoi bitch's moult is often quite profuse (compared with a dog's), the coat should be quite long and silky, either flat, wavy or curly, ample tail feathering being particularly desirable.

Be sure you get your prospect to stand so that you can walk around her assessing her balance and stance. Ensure good overall body linkage, i.e. how the various parts couple, quarters to body, set-on of tail, neck to body, head to neck and so on. The neck, seen from the side will reveal if the head is held nobly as it should be. Sometimes, when the shoulder formation is faulty, i.e. too upright, the neck will be held too low and the head thrust forward rather than held high. Look at her feet—if they are too spread and flat she will not move well when you come to see her in action. In fact, it is an interesting and worthwhile exercise just before you see her in action to wager with yourself how you *think* she will move from what you have seen of her body features standing.

Finally, you *must* see the bitch in action. This should be arranged so that a competent handler can move her at varying speeds from a walk to a fast trot. Any deficiencies in her soundness should become apparent during these exercises and you will then be in a position to confirm your decision. Stand at one end of the arena where the bitch is to be moved. Let her be taken directly away from you in a straight line. Remember, the Borzoi's hindquarters are singularly adapted to take the dog off at great speed and with bounding agility which can be redirected suddenly at will. However, the dog being on a leash will be unable to express her entire repertoire of speed and you must assess her hind action as you see it. This means that action or gait, as it is sometimes termed should be 'straight and true'. The hind legs must go away well separated one from the other, moving in their own track, the action being firm, positive and sound. There must be no suggestion of action being 'close-behind' which is a show term indicating that a dog's hind feet are kept together in movement closer than is correct. Another fault is when one hind leg kicking out sideways, suggests some structural weakness at the hip. Action *must* be springy and free.

The bitch should then be brought towards you. The action in this case must be positive, the legs being picked-up well and not 'paddled' or 'plaited', i.e. with one fore arm passed over or nearly over the other as the dog comes towards you. High, proud action in a dog or bitch is acceptable in the Borzoi world so long as it does not embrace a short stride or mincing gait. The whole aspect of the Borzoi is to show movement which is long-reaching, positive and therefore highly effective when coursing. Consequently, every muscle contributes to the end result and although we in Britain cannot use our dog to perform against his natural quarry, the wolf, we have to consider his worth and qualities with this end in mind.

You have given your bitch a pretty good overhauling. If she conforms to your requirements and the personal approval of the expert you have brought with you, then buy her, for she should be right. Thank the vendor for being so patient and acquiescent to your buying whims and take home your investment.

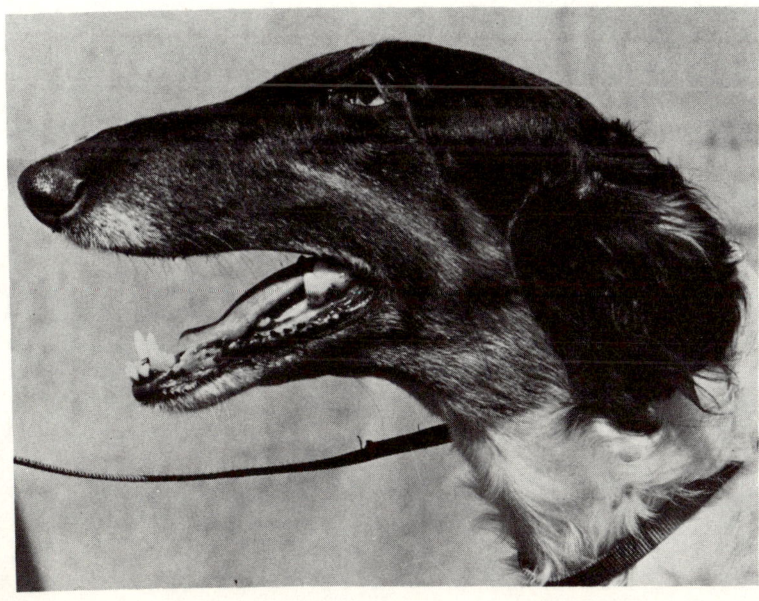

Mrs. E. Etheridge's Rodgivad Virago
Photo: Levinson

The Dog

As the dog you are likely to use with your bitch will probably belong to someone else, you are free to take your time finding him as in this instance you should have many dogs to choose from. *Never* use an untried dog at stud. You might fancy your chances as an assessor of canine virtues in the blood, but you need to be little more than a magician to 'hit the jackpot' with such a sire. It is better to let someone else try him first—then you can look at his puppies (taking into consideration their dam), and judge better his propensities.

Always choose a stud dog on his record as a stud dog. This means his get or progeny brand him as good or bad at the job. A show dog with all the cards and ribbons a winner can muster in his brief term on the show bench should never influence you. Much of his winning can be worthless, taken in classes where the competition is sparse, or mediocre. Many a champion has won his third and deciding challenge certificate at some out-of-the-way championship show which is invariably poorly supported by the usual show-going crowd. Plenty of first prizes are very nice, but they do not do much more than tell you the Borzoi is probably a good specimen in himself—a handsome one, no doubt, but it does not tell you what good he can do to his breed. The 'good' that comes from a dog is in what he can produce and by the value of a dog's progeny so is his name made and impressed in the annals of his breed.

Do not think that because your bitch is deficient in one department or the other that her fault or faults can be corrected at once by putting her to a dog who is strong in the features she lacks. The primary task is to make yourself aware of the weak points in her make-up. Unless you do this and freely accept her faults you will never correct them. Any fault can be bred out of a strain, given time, care and prudent calculation. What you have to guard against is not to breed in other faults hitherto unknown to the strain while you are dispersing those you know about!

So look for a dog who is a real Borzoi. He must be handsome, upstanding, masculine and quite typical, certainly conforming closely to the breed Standard. Find this kind of sire and then look around at the litters he has produced, preferably young sons and daughters of his who have reached the yearling stage. Assuming they look good and that some are winning already in the show circuits, then you may have the dog you seek—provided, of course, that he lines up satisfactorily with your bitch in the very important matters of their respective breeding. Take *his* pedigree and do with it what you did with the bitch's—fill in the description of those of his ancestors about whom you can obtain data. Then with the dog's dossier placed above that of the bitch, compare them point by point, ancestor with ancestor. If line-breeding is to be your plan of campaign, then you must find at least within the first four generations the name of a beautiful and noted Borzoi worth breeding to. His name should appear as a common denominator to both pedigrees. In the following example Ch. 'Tom' is the name of the 'beautiful and noted' Borzoi you will breed to, although you could just as effectively line-breed to a worthwhile bitch:

Parents	G.-Parents	G.G.-Parents	G.G.G.-Parents
The Stud Dog	Percy	Peter	William
			Mary
		Maria	Frank
			Rose
	Polly	**Ch. Tom**	Ch. Billy
			Andrea
		Bessie	Bonzo
			Doris

(For the purpose of this example all names shown are fictitious)

Parents	G.-Parents	G.G.-Parents	G.G.G.-Parents
Your Bitch	Jason	Bernard	Albert
			Ellen
		Freda	George
			Eva
	Tricia	**Ch. Tom**	Ch. Billy
			Andrea
		Bessie	Leonard
			Pearl

Make absolutely certain that the stud dog possesses an ideal temperament. If he did most of his winning under judges who qualify as Borzoi specialists it is highly probable that he will be a dog of the right disposition for Borzoi people realize the need for maintaining it. A Borzoi lacking true breed temperament is only 'half' a dog and certainly not one to be used in building up a new strain.

The Mating

It is assumed that your bitch is ready for taking on maternal duties, which means that not only should she be of reasonably mature physical proportions, but past her first 'heat' or season. This infers that she will be about fifteen months of age or older. You will presumably have a fairly good idea as to when her next heat is due. It is best to advise the stud dog owner that you propose using his dog and then later when she nears her time of season give him adequate warning of the date. Once she begins to show 'colour' which is a bright blood discharge at the mouth of the vulva (which will have swollen a little a few days earlier followed by an intermediary pinkish secretion), you will know she is shortly to be ready for mating. The term is usually between ten and fourteen days from the commencement of the initial discharge by which time all signs of blood will have dispersed, although the actual oestrum or season itself lasts usually about three weeks.

Bitches vary enormously in their preferred day for mating. Some will receive a dog any time between the tenth and fourteenth day, even a little earlier or later, others seem to like more specific days. These have to be catered for or you will never get them mated and if you learn by experience that your bitch is one to be mated on say the eleventh day of her heat, then you must ensure that you book her to the stud dog for just that day— no other will do. Another type of bitch, and this sort is rather a nuisance, becomes ripe for mating over a very short span of time, sometimes only a few hours in their season. It is not always easy to catch them at this time and the answer seems to be that both dog and bitch should be kennelled in adjoining runs. Then when the bitch is ready for the dog she will indicate this in the usual manner and the dog can be introduced at once. Such an arrangement is rather trying to the stud dog who will be 'teased' to his disadvantage perhaps for many hours before he can get to the bitch. Needless to add, not many stud dog owners like bitches of this kind either and if you have such a female you might find extra fees and/or charges to pay for the inconvenience she causes at the visited kennel.

It is usual for the bitch to visit the dog, although some stud dog owners do not mind doing it the other way round so long as you pay fares, etc. Often enough it suits the bitch herself better to be mated on her own territory and the job is accomplished with minimum delay. However, if you take your charge to the dog, try and arrange it so that the union can be effected fairly early in the morning. Incidentally, always try and accompany your bitch to the dog. No bitch should be railed a long distance to arrive in strange surroundings and find herself involved with a dog whom she may well not like. She will be, most probably, in a very nervous state being in season and a bitch in a distressed frame of mind is liable to 'miss' even following a good mating. This means you will have to wait at least another six months before you can try again, quite apart from the expense involved. Further, if you are present at the scene of the mating you can come away feeling satisfied that the dog in use was the one of your choice and that you saw things through from start to finish.

Ensure that both animals have had a free run around with ample time to attend to their natural functions. Usually if the stud dog is an experienced animal he will lose little time in making overtures. It is best to have both dogs on their respective leashes during the introductions; this will allow the bitch to be edged away from him if she grabs at him in annoyance. It may seem prudent to present her to him rear end first, when his attentions will soon excite her. If you and the stud dog owner feel that the pair will get on well together they can be released and watched closely as they run free. Never leave a mating pair unattended, although if you listen to some breeders they seem to prefer a 'natural' mating. This entails dog and bitch being left alone to conduct affairs unaided and in their own way. Sometimes the pair do effect copulation without much ado and of course, if this happens it is ideal. However, more often than not, there is a skirmish or two before the dog can enter the bitch and even when entry has been effected and a 'tie' made, a fidgety and impatient bitch can do a dog and herself a good deal of harm.

The stud dog's natural instinct will make him take the initiative and mount the bitch from behind. He will at once begin to thrust at her and an experienced male will soon enter. Once this has been noted, the stud dog owner should come behind him and steady the dog squarely and firmly against the bitch's rear while you should hold your bitch's head firmly by clasping on either side of her neck. This will not only give her confidence and re-assurance at your presence but prevent her from swinging round at the crucial moment and trying to dis- lodge the dog. If matters proceed well a 'tie' will soon be achieved, meaning that seminal fluid is being deposited and that a proper mating can be assumed. To explain the 'tie' quite briefly, this is caused by a bulb situated in the dog's penis. This becomes engorged with blood as the penis erects and swells to several times its normal size. It is then held securely and firmly in position by the sphincter muscle of the bitch's vagina, thereby locking both animals together. It is best, if this can be managed, to turn the pair tail-to-tail for their own comfort while the mating lasts. This can be achieved by lifting the dog carefully so that his forelegs can be brought off the bitch's back and put to the ground beside her. Then taking one of his hind legs, gently lift it over the bitch's back at the same time swivelling him round and away from her. This will culminate in their heads pointing different ways but the pair will remain 'tied'. Such unions last from a few minutes even up to an hour and a half, but the usual time is twenty minutes. The mating pair should be watched meanwhile until they come apart as towards the end of the union, either or both will begin to fidget. Once parted, the dog should be removed from the bitch's presence and his comfort attended to by ensuring that his sheath has returned to the correct position over the penis. The bitch should be dried over at the back and both animals can then be allowed to drink, and fed, if necessary, a little later. If you notice that seminal fluid appears to have been spilled, do not worry. It is likely that much more spermatozoa than seems wasted will have been deposited into the bitch's vagina, and when it is remembered that in one mating many millions of sperms are released the chances of a 'miss' (failure to conceive) are slight. This presumes, of course, that all other factors are good and normal.

At this point, it is interesting perhaps to consider the tail-to-tail natural mating position of dogs (and other animals so provided for by Nature). In the wild state, a mating pair having their biting jaws or armament at either end would be in a position for strategic turning in a complete circle should they be attacked at such an inconvenient time. They would be far less vulnerable, therefore, than were both their backs turned the same way.

Some breeders prefer to have their bitch mated twice by the stud dog. This seems to give them added confidence that the bitch will 'take' and prove successful in having puppies. With a stud dog in regular use, this is quite unnecessary if the initial mating was a good one. With a dog never before used at stud, an elderly male, or one seldom used, it can be a good idea, in this case the second union should follow the first within twenty hours. The idea behind this is that the second service will be stimulated by the first in the cases of such stud dogs just referred to. It is a dubious belief. Remember that most Borzoi are virile and things seldom go wrong if their mating is handled expertly, therefore, it is a good idea to get a young dog stud 'shown the ropes' at say ten months of age by a matron bitch whose receptive manner at mating time will give him confidence. Once he has had a stud job, it is best to let him rest until he has a second bitch at say, fifteen months of age. Then from two years onwards

Mr. R. A. Bassett's Ch. Grand Manner of Colhugh

he can start his stud career in earnest. However, keep a close eye on him to ensure that he maintains good condition. He will need plenty of fresh, raw meat feeding, ample protein and so on if he is going to keep in good bloom. Never expect too much sense at mating time from a dog who has been celibate for some years. Often a dog of this category has no idea what to do when he is introduced to a bitch in full heat. Such dogs, if they are worth using may need a good deal of re-assurance and perhaps manipulative assistance in order to effect a proper mating.

Pre-natal Care

Borzois do not easily reveal to the eye that they are in whelp until quite near the end of the normal term of gestation which is sixty-three days. However, it is very important to start preparing for the hoped-for litter and the bitch's prime condition must be her owner's first thought. She must be exercised quite normally every day and groomed in the usual way, but guided well away from any activity which might prove harmful such as fighting, falling into the river and so on. Admittedly, she might well do all these things were she in the wild state, but she is a domestic creature these days and conditioned to an easier way of life. She will need worming perhaps and this can be discussed with your veterinary surgeon, although there are many reliable remedies on the market these days. The vet will advise also in the matter of injections. The modern bitch is beset with a number of infections which fall mainly into the streptococcal and staphylococcal categories. Your professional man will know what to do to avoid fading puppies, i.e. whelps which die eventually after a miserable week's life, also absorption, when no puppies arrive after what appears a normal pregnancy. However, these are dangers which you might never become involved with.

Mrs. M. Malone's Ch. Petroff of Enolam

Borzoi litters are frequently big—sometimes as many as a dozen, but from five to ten is normal. This means that not only the dam, but the whelps she is carrying need building up. This can be achieved not only with good and perhaps improved feeding, but with extra nourishment including calcium phosphate sources, especially plenty of milk.

Prepare a whelping box or suitable place for her. If a box (such as is shown in the sketch) make sure that it is very big and roomy. If she has the maximum number of puppies, then space will be limited. The box should allow room for the dam with her puppies to lie down in comfort. The 'pig-rail' shown will permit a small puppy some protection from being squashed by a clumsy mother and the front can be let-down for easy access and exit if required. A piece of laundered and disinfected hessian is ideal for affixing to the bottom of the box, but until the bitch has had her puppies and has settled down with them it is as well to let her do the actual whelping either on the bare board of the base or on newspapers which are particularly ideal for they can be gathered up and disposed of at will, also replaced immediately with clean ones. The bitch should be introduced to her new quarters about ten days before she is due to whelp. Do not expect her to react kindly to the idea if you delay this until a few hours before her litter arrives. She will have enough to think about at this time without having the distraction of a strange bed to consider. Never use straw or blankets in the whelping box. The puppies crawl out of sight underneath and are in danger of being squashed if the bitch cannot see them.

Make sure that you have informed your veterinary surgeon the expected date of whelping. You might need him in an emergency and he will then be ready for any urgent call.

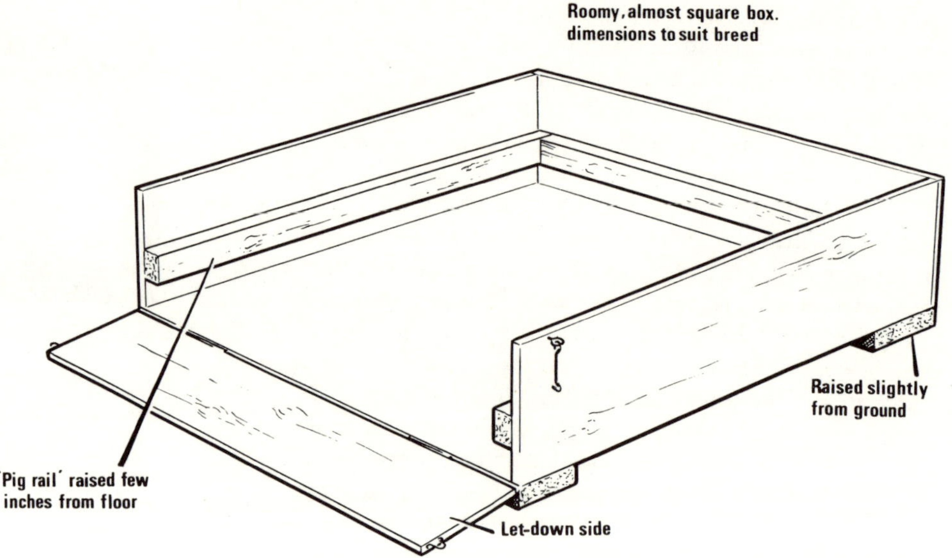

The Whelping

As the time for having her puppies draws closer you will observe the bitch becomes steadily less relaxed, until just prior to the actual whelping when she will show every sign of restlessness, even some agitation. This will involve some turning around on herself, sudden 'braking' when moving and clear indication of worry, more evident in a maiden bitch than one who has experienced it all before. These symptoms are often evinced for two or three days prior to the actual day of whelping by which time her temperature which is normally 101·4°F will have dropped to 100°F or 97·5°F when she is about to deliver her young. A cautious breeder will find this a good and safe guide warning him that labour is about to commence.

Table showing when a bitch is due to whelp

Served Jan.	Whelps March	Served Feb.	Whelps April	Served March	Whelps May	Served April	Whelps June	Served May	Whelps July	Served June	Whelps Aug.	Served July	Whelps Sept.	Served Aug.	Whelps Oct.	Served Sept.	Whelps Nov.	Served Oct.	Whelps Dec.	Served Nov.	Whelps Jan.	Served Dec.	Whelps Feb.
1	5	1	5	1	3	1	3	1	3	1	3	1	2	1	3	1	3	1	3	1	3	1	2
2	6	2	6	2	4	2	4	2	4	2	4	2	3	2	4	2	4	2	4	2	4	2	3
3	7	3	7	3	5	3	5	3	5	3	5	3	4	3	5	3	5	3	5	3	5	3	4
4	8	4	8	4	6	4	6	4	6	4	6	4	5	4	6	4	6	4	6	4	6	4	5
5	9	5	9	5	7	5	7	5	7	5	7	5	6	5	7	5	7	5	7	5	7	5	6
6	10	6	10	6	8	6	8	6	8	6	8	6	7	6	8	6	8	6	8	6	8	6	7
7	11	7	11	7	9	7	9	7	9	7	9	7	8	7	9	7	9	7	9	7	9	7	8
8	12	8	12	8	10	8	10	8	10	8	10	8	9	8	10	8	10	8	10	8	10	8	9
9	13	9	13	9	11	9	11	9	11	9	11	9	10	9	11	9	11	9	11	9	11	9	10
10	14	10	14	10	12	10	12	10	12	10	12	10	11	10	12	10	12	10	12	10	12	10	11
11	15	11	15	11	13	11	13	11	13	11	13	11	12	11	13	11	13	11	13	11	13	11	12
12	16	12	16	12	14	12	14	12	14	12	14	12	13	12	14	12	14	12	14	12	14	12	13
13	17	13	17	13	15	13	15	13	15	13	15	13	14	13	15	13	15	13	15	13	15	13	14
14	18	14	18	14	16	14	16	14	16	14	16	14	15	14	16	14	16	14	16	14	16	14	15
15	19	15	19	15	17	15	17	15	17	15	17	15	16	15	17	15	17	15	17	15	17	15	16
16	20	16	20	16	18	16	18	16	18	16	18	16	17	16	18	16	18	16	18	16	18	16	17
17	21	17	21	17	19	17	19	17	19	17	19	17	18	17	19	17	19	17	19	17	19	17	18
18	22	18	22	18	20	18	20	18	20	18	20	18	19	18	20	18	20	18	20	18	20	18	19
19	23	19	23	19	21	19	21	19	21	19	20	19	20	19	21	19	21	19	21	19	21	19	20
20	24	20	24	20	22	20	22	20	22	20	21	20	21	20	22	20	22	20	22	20	22	20	21
21	25	21	25	21	23	21	23	21	23	21	22	21	22	21	23	21	23	21	23	21	23	21	22
22	26	22	26	22	24	22	24	22	24	22	23	22	23	22	24	22	24	22	24	22	24	22	23
23	27	23	27	23	25	23	25	23	25	23	24	23	24	23	25	23	25	23	25	23	25	23	24
24	28	24	28	24	26	24	26	24	26	24	25	24	25	24	26	24	26	24	26	24	26	24	25
25	29	25	29	25	27	25	27	25	27	25	26	25	26	25	27	25	27	25	27	25	27	25	26
26	30	26	30	26	28	26	28	26	28	26	27	26	27	26	28	26	28	26	28	26	28	26	27
27	31	27	1	27	29	27	29	27	29	27	28	27	28	27	29	27	29	27	29	27	29	27	28
28	1	28	2	28	30	28	30	28	30	28	29	28	29	28	30	22	30	28	30	28	30	28	1
29	2	29	3	29	31	29	1	29	31	29	30	29	30	29	31	29	1	29	31	29	31	29	2
30	3			30	1	30	2	30	1	30	1	30	1	30	1	30	2	30	1	30	1	30	3
31	4			31	2			31	2			31	2	31	2			31	2			31	4

The bitch will probably refuse all meals just prior to whelping, when she will repose into a deep sleep which will set her up well for the coming ardours of the whelping. It should be arranged, when you see her in this state, that she is left well alone and not in any way distracted by strangers or other dogs, even those well known to her. The room temperature should be not less than 70°F.

When the bitch awakens, she will probably be ready to start whelping and this will be intimated by scratching at the floor of her box and by general restlessness. You should have ready by you in the whelping room, a number of first-aid items to include:

(a) Paper tissues.
(b) Surgical lint cut into 10-inch squares or useful size.
(c) Sharp, probe-pointed surgical scissors, sterilized.
(d) Surgical cotton, cut to pieces about 6 inches long.
(e) An antiseptic/disinfectant.
(f) Petroleum jelly in tube or jar.
(g) Supply of cotton wool.
(h) Odd pieces of clean washed towelling or face flannels.

(*i*) Hot water bottle (old fashioned stone variety best) covered with cloth or sock for protection.

(*j*) Feeding bottle or pipette.

(*k*) Kettle of water, ready plugged in to mains or on gas; box of matches.

(*l*) Brandy, small teaspoon. This is either for bitch, her puppies (in which case absolute minimal measures to be given) or yourself!

(*m*) General food and sustenance for yourself.

(*n*) Plenty of old newspapers.

(*o*) Basin.

Obviously, you can make your own selection of these requisites, but the purpose of the exercise is that you should be ready with the things you want rather than search around for them at a time when your presence may well be better employed alongside your bitch while whelping.

The bitch will soon commence to strain, the periods of labour becoming more frequent as she gets near to delivering her first puppy. If you think it prudent, offer her a little warm milk. She may or may not take it, but it does so often have the effect of hastening the arrival of her first-born. However, it is usually better to leave her well alone—do not feed her, do not talk to her, just let her get on with the task. If everything proceeds properly, a small water-filled bag will appear at the mouth of the vulva. This is a sort of cushion or buffer which will protect the oncoming puppy when it greets the outside world. The bitch's muscular contractions will eventually rend the bag, the puppy soon follows in a membraneous sac, head first. The bitch, with vigorous licking, will break the sac, releasing the puppy together with a good deal of fluid, which will be soaked-up by the newspapers lining the whelping box. The puppy, following its buffeting by the bitch's tongue will soon commence to breathe, even squeak with apparent peevishness. It will be attached by its umbilical cord to the afterbirth (placenta) and the bitch will, instinctively, sever the cord close to the whelp's navel with a sharp nip. If she seems unable or disinclined to conduct this operation it must be done for her. Take one of the ready-prepared short lengths of surgical thread and tie it tightly round the cord about an inch up the umbilical cord from the puppy's navel. Then cut the cord with the sterilized scissors about one inch above the tie you have made. Sometimes the bitch will devour the afterbirth and if this happens, so well and good, it will do her no harm as it is a perfectly natural action. If she does not eat it then dispose of it for her. Sometimes the afterbirth remains in the womb when it will have to be withdrawn gently, or it will decompose and cause what will probably amount to a septic condition. The withdrawal can be effected by drawing carefully and directly on the hanging cord until it is quite free from the bitch's body.

The first puppy is sometimes a long while appearing, although Borzoi puppies generally breed easily as they are 'streamlined' in head and body. However, if a puppy is stubborn in coming through or its position seems an abnormal one, then it may need assistance. Breech births are easy enough to deal with, i.e. when the feet or rear end is presented first, in which case the part to be seen is gripped gently with one of the towel pieces you have ready and the puppy is withdrawn without ado. Make sure if you have to do this that you do it with all speed if the bag is already broken, but take care that you do not squeeze the whelp's body in your anxiety. Try and effect the withdrawal in rhythm with the natural straining of the dam, but effective speed at such a time is of great importance. If you feel doubtful as to your ability to perform such a task, then it is better to call in your veterinary surgeon when this need arises. He will also be able to deal with any retained placenta with an injection of Pituitrin.

The bitch will usually sleep or doze between deliveries and this should be encouraged as she is gathering her energies in this way. Usually, if she has managed to deliver three without trouble the rest will follow automatically, the intervals between puppies varying often quite considerably. As she progresses you should try and find opportunities for clearing up. Large dogs such as the Borzoi make quite a lot of mess when whelping, especially with the bulk of water which is released at every birth. Once the bitch seems to have finished, try and get her to go outside and relieve herself and give her a bowl of warm milk to encourage her. Once outside you can commence a quick tidy-up, putting the puppies into a basket near by and disposing at once of the soiled newspapers. Check every puppy for its sex and make sure no abnormalities exist. Provided you are satisfied that there are no more puppies to come, you can leave the bitch to her own devices for a while which will give you a chance to compose yourself. However, if you are in any doubt then the opinion of your veterinary surgeon should be sought, although once a bitch has settled down and the puppies are sucking away merrily at her there is very little chance of further births and all should be well.

The most useful size of litter is from five to seven. A Borzoi, although able to cope with more will make the best of seven and such a number is really enough for any dam. If you have a larger litter than this, you may consider culling or using a foster mother. Foster mothers are often advertised in the canine Press. Certain kennels specialize in supplying good clean bitches (often Collies) for the purpose. If you have say, a litter of nine Borzois, you can put five on to the natural dam, four on to the

Collie and you should get maximum results. However, for the first four days it is best to keep the entire litter on the Borzoi, for then they will *all* get the benefit of her initial milk flow, which contains Colostrum, an antibiotic which is of prime value to them. Make sure that every puppy is given a fair share of the feeding. The inguinal teats are most plenteous in their supply. These are the large teats in the lower regions and you should make sure that each puppy is placed down here in his turn and watched so that he is not pushed off by greedier members of the litter. In the initial stages, the bitch can be fed with a sustaining drink of warm milk to which a teaspoonful of glucose or a dessertspoonful of honey has been added. She should have plenty of milk to drink as this will aid and build up her own milk supply.

Post-Whelping Problems

Eclampsia

This is a common occurrence after whelping, although it can happen shortly before a bitch delivers her puppies. It is a sort of milk fever and brings on restlessness and nervousness, accompanied by panting. The condition is caused by a deficiency of

Mrs. J. L. Gibbs' Opal of Fortrouge and Mrs. N. Sanderson's Sholwood Silvermere
Photo: Gibbs

calcium and vitamin D. The matter can be rectified with injections of calcium in the form of Collo-Cal-D preparation. Keep an eye on dam and puppies every hour after whelping. Eclampsia can occur even three or four weeks after the date of the puppies' arrival and the danger period is not over until after weaning has been completed.

Aglactia

This is lack of milk and it is a condition quite common in modern bitches. The dam suddenly acquires a high temperature and this prevents her milk passing through the teats to her puppies. She often panics and the puppies make their displeasure quite audible! The condition persists as a rule for two to three days, which is rather worrying as a milk flow in the initial stages is important. During this period the milk contains Colostrum. which is not only a mild laxative, but is highly nourishing being well endowed with protein. It may act also as an antibiotic to the puppy in the first few weeks of his life. Consequently, the fact that its effect can be lost to the puppy is a worrying one.

The bitch will often improve after just a few hours of suffering this distressing condition, and she can be helped by continually pressing the puppies to her teats. However, if this proves of no

Mr. and Mrs. R. Searle's Ch. Francehill Diamond Lil

avail, call in the veterinary surgeon. He will inject the bitch, thereby reducing her temperature and once returned to normal body heat the milk will flow normally and the puppies feed and thrive happily.

Metritis

This is a condition usually due to retention of the last born puppy's placenta in the dam's womb, although it can be caused by even small particles of membrane which have been left behind. There is often an unpleasant septic discharge from the vulva and the bitch will appear in considerable discomfort, the milk flow being disrupted and the puppies clearly indisposed. Inflammation of the uterus is usually noted about a week after the whelping and the bitch's temperature and pulse rate will be high. Urgent attention to the matter is important and the veterinary surgeon may well have to act immediately in order to save her. Naturally, a bitch in this state will be unable to care for her puppies properly and the entire litter will have to be removed and either put to a foster dam or hand-reared.

Hand-rearing

This is by no means an easy task. It requires immense patience and the person doing it needs to be dedicated to the task. The entire litter has to be fed as one, i.e. no individual puppy (unless he is a weakling) can be treated different from his brother or sister. The weakling may need extra attention, although frankly, if the litter to be hand-reared is but a day or so old and there is a weakling involved, then it is better and kinder to have it painlessly destroyed. 'Lactol' is a good substitute for bitch's milk, although there is no true substitute for the real thing. Mixing instructions and how to hand-rear will be found on the canister, and great care should be taken to ensure that these are followed. It is just as important to keep to precise quantities of food, and to exact times of feeding. Temperature of the food is another feature of vital importance and fresh food is necessary at every meal-time. There are a number of ways of administering the food to a small puppy, but care must be taken neither to over-feed nor to feed too fast. Keep the cup of 'Lactol' mixture in a bowl of warm water so that the temperature of the food can be maintained and this will ensure that when the last puppy in the litter comes to be fed, his food will be at the same correct temperature as the first member receiving his food. A good guide as to whether the youngsters are being fed properly and are content can be taken from their attitude. Happy puppies will settle down to sleep after they have been fed and cleaned-up. Unsettled youngsters will cry inces-

Miss B. Murray's Ch. Zircon of Fortrouge

santly and pass motions which instead of being of firm porridge-like consistency and brown in colour are loose and yellow. Such indications as these are sufficient to warn the hand-rearer that the mixture he is feeding the puppies is too strong and needs diluting. The youngsters should be weighed daily and exact records kept and each one examined closely to ensure its progressively good condition.

Once a puppy has been fed, wipe his face and especially his nose and lips with a swab of damp cotton wool. This will remove milk which has settled there following his feed and prevent any waste from congealing. The dam, if she were present, would keep her puppies clean, and lick and buffet them a little around their genitals and rear parts to induce urination and the passing of motions. This action must therefore be dealt with artificially, and this can be done by soaking a wad of cotton wool in *warm* water and stroking their private parts gently with this. Once the motions have been passed, smear a little petroleum jelly around each anus and penis or vulva as the case may be. No puppy should be allowed to remain constipated. In one so young this can prove fatal. If any youngster fails to pass his main motion following his meal, grease a veterinary thermometer and insert it fractionally into the rectum. This will invariably cause the required motion.

It is a good idea to instal an infra-red lamp when you are maintaining an orphan litter, deprived of its dam's body warmth. These lamps are today freely available from the better pet shops or can be seen advertised in the canine weeklies. An infra-red lamp should be suspended from the ceiling and set to produce a constant temperature of between 75°–80°, at least for the first three days. After this, the heat can be reduced to 60° but this must be done gradually and this is achieved by raising the lamp a little each day. A dull-emitter bulb should be used, this being considered harmless to the youngsters' eyes when they open about ten days after birth. Place a wire guard round the lamp reflector to give added security, in case a bulb should inadvertently break loose and fall to the ground.

In spite of the time you will spend in hand-rearing, the sleep you cannot fail to lose in the process, you will experience a great and lasting satisfaction when the job is complete and you will realize how wonderfully fit and well look the litter of Borzois you *might* have lost.

Dewclaws

The dewclaw is the rudimentary fifth digit which is equivalent to the thumb in a human. It appears on the insides of the puppy's forelegs, just above the feet. Sometimes dewclaws will be noted on the hind limbs too, and these are particularly

Mrs. L. Pearson's and Mr. K. L. Prior's Ch. Zomahli Harorshyi

Mrs. J. Bennett-Heard's Ch. Reyas Keepers Kwango

objectionable. Remove them all when the puppy is about four days old, as if left they can prove a nuisance to their owner in later life by getting entangled and becoming torn. The operation can be effected by a competent breeder, although most people prefer a veterinary surgeon to do it. If you do it, use a pair of sharp, snub-nosed surgical scissors making a swift cut, then brush in or dab on with cotton wool some permanganate of potash to stem the bleeding.

The wounds should be examined at least once a day until they have healed.

Chapter 5

Feeding

Weaning and Puppy Feeding

How well you wean your puppies will decide much as to their future health and appearance. The dam will normally take responsibility for their milk up to say the age of one month, but if she has had a big litter to care for, she is likely to need some assistance by the time her family is three weeks old. This assumes that the bitch's milk has been adequate in volume and of good quality. It will soon become apparent from her puppies' coat and condition if either of these factors is at fault and you will then have to start weaning very early. However, bitch's milk is essential to the brood while they can get it and no other milk compares with it—as far as puppies are concerned, of course. In *The Complete Dog Breeder's Manual*, 1954, by Clifford Hubbard, the author gives an interesting table which reveals the difference between the milk of a bitch and that of four other familiar animals. The table is as follows:

Analyses of Milk

Animal	Sugar	Casein, etc.	Fat	Salts	Water
Dog	3·1	8·0	12·0	1·2	75·5
Goat	4·75	4·0	6·25	1·0	84·0
Cat	5·2	7·9	3·65	0·9	82·35
Cow	4·85	3·75	3·7	0·6	87·1
Sheep	4·95	4·7	5·2	0·7	84·45

'Lactol' is excellent for weaning and can be prepared as a substitute for bitch's milk. Instructions will be found with the preparation, careful reference being taken as to the age of the youngsters. The milk is normally fed at blood heat and as with hand-rearing, the mixture should be stood in a cup which in turn is stood in a bowl of hot water. This will ensure that the first and last puppy in the litter are fed at the same heat. It is not difficult to get a small puppy to lap, just smear a little of the preparation under his lips and wait for it to be taken in. At first progress will be slow, but once the youngster gets the taste he will start lapping with enthusiasm. Every puppy has to be fed individually at first and once you have them all lapping with confidence they can be introduced to a communal feeding dish. By this time the dam's personal burden of feeding has been eased a little and although her puppies will still be at her teats, at least they will not be dragging at her excessively. Before putting down the feeding bowl, make sure they have not been near their dam for an hour or more previously. They will then approach their prepared meal with good appetites. Borzoi puppies are not gluttons like some breeds' youngsters, but exceptions do occur. The average puppy can be left to get on with his meal without hogging from his fellows, but the exception referred to may need controlling, so watch them all the time when eating. Try and keep the feeding trough at a raised level, i.e. a little off the ground. This will ensure that the puppies will not fall into the food and it will aid towards a better head posture and improve the youngsters' general bearing.

Feeding can be stepped up from the 'Lactol' routine after three or four days. The extra diet can include minced boiled tripe, poached egg and light milk puddings also finely shredded or minced raw fresh meat. The meat should be introduced in easy stages, but the quantity should be increased gradually until it represents about 50 per cent of the intake. Care should be taken that not too much food is put down at a time. To avoid distension and digestive discomforts, it is best to divide a normal daily intake into four or five 'sittings', spread over a twelve hour period. By the time the puppies are six weeks old they will have become quite big and at this age they will be increasing in weight to the extent of nearly 3 lb. a week. About this time, maybe even earlier, the dam herself will be disgorging some of her food for the puppies' benefit. This is a natural action and need not perturb a breeder who has not witnessed it before, but its advantages are mixed. The puppies will rush at the partly-digested food and gobble it up, so you should make sure that the meals you give the dam at this time do not contain either food which is too rich for puppies or cut up too large for their gullets. Also, if the dam is allowed to disgorge food too often she is going to fall badly out of condition and this is the wrong time for that to happen. In fact, she must now be built up well with high protein food with plenty of fresh raw meat, although fluids can be cut down severely as her milk supply must be minimal.

Mrs. M. Malone's Ch. Black Limelight of Enolam

The puppies themselves should be drinking plenty of milk, however, as milk is essential for their good growth and bone. At six weeks of age they will be on four meals a day, two meat meals and two milky feeds, given to them alternately. By now they should be quite independent of their dam's milk supply, even her presence. The amount of food will need increasing and the way it is measured also the quality will determine their development in the next few months. Do not over-stuff them and this is why it is important to keep an eye on feeding Borzoi puppies, from which you will soon gain an intimate knowledge of each puppy's requirements and learn much of his eating idiosyncrasies. In the next week you can reduce the actual number of meals to three but this does not mean the quantity has to be reduced, quite the opposite, in fact, for as a puppy grows, he needs more.

During the whole of the puppy-rearing term from weaning to complete independence, it is important to inspect every youngster after his meal. The nose and mouth will need wiping over to obviate waste food encrustment and the under-tail area and the genitals should be examined after motions have been passed and cleaned-up if necessary.

Worming

As this is a matter which requires attention during the weaning period it can be included in this section. The commonly encountered worm in puppies is the roundworm. This is a parasite rather like vermicelli and creamy-white in colour, and all puppies are thought to be infested in greater or lesser degree. The dam herself probably passes them on to her embryonic young but they are easily enough acquired by puppies from the faeces of infected dogs, or from eggs which are taken orally from their dam's teats in course of feeding.

The infested puppy seldom thrives until the pest has been eradicated. His appetite usually falls off, although instances have been noted when an appetite has become ravenous. The coat inclines to 'stare' and divide, while motions seem 'jellied' or very loose, indicating an upset stomach. There are many good proprietary vermifuges and vermicides on the market today and the average owner prefers to use one of these quite early in the youngster's life. At one time it was not considered prudent to worm a puppy before it was at least five weeks old, but veterinary medicine now permits earlier dosing with no ill-effects. For those who do not fancy the task of worming their puppies, the veterinary surgeon will attend to the matter for a nominal fee. When expelled (if a vermifuge is used) the worms will appear in a tightly-knit skein and will probably surprise you by their number. Burn them at once and disinfect the area of

Mrs. E. Ruggles' Dougal of Matalona
Photo: Diane Pearce

operations, at the same time cleaning up the now relieved puppy in his anal region.

The tapeworm is rather different. It attachs itself by a sort of hook to the intestinal wall and is made up with a number of segments small at the head end, but gradually increasing in size towards the 'tail', or opposite end. Each segment is really a worm in its own right and on breaking away from the main stem and being passed through its host becomes ingested by an animal such as the sheep, horse, rabbit or fox. A flea can pass on the worm to the dog who can also acquire the parasite from the viscera of an infected produce animal or caught rabbit.

This worm is less frequently met with than the roundworm, but its effect is rather less pleasant. It can be noted, as a rule when the grain-like segments which comprise the main shaft of the worm are seen adhering to the dog's anus or are evident in his motions. It is best to ask your vet to deal with this worm as he is more likely to do this effectively (it being quite often several feet in length), than you would with a home remedy. Once expelled, the dog's condition will improve noticeably within a few days, his coat will become glossy and healthy and the strong body and breath odours, usually so evident in dogs with tapeworm, will disappear.

Note that every puppy before being sold should be wormed (for roundworm) and this should be done at least three days before he goes. The breeder should make sure that the worming has not affected adversely the youngster's stomach and that his motions are firm and healthy by the time he reaches his new home and owner.

Mrs. W. Chadwick's Ch. Winjones Razluka

Winjones Borzois at exercise

Adult Feeding

One is inclined perhaps to consider what the dog would eat were he in the wild state. This may be a useful guide to feeding, but the findings should not be followed slavishly as it must be realized the dog today is not wild, but domesticated and his modified chemical make-up as such governs to a large extent his particular requirements.

However, it is important that he has fresh raw meat as his main and staple diet. By all means get him used to eating lightly cooked meat, canned proprietary dog foods, carefully boned steamed white fish and so on. However, do this selfishly because it will be more convenient for you as his owner to feed him with this provender (however excellent it may be) if you cannot lay your hands on the fresh raw meat. Too many dogs today having been fed solely on meat will refuse all other kinds of food and such a dog can prove a worry to his owner at times. A dog prefers his meat in large lumps so he can tear off the pieces he wants to eat and enjoy it at will. Few dog owners feed their dogs in this way, preferring to cut up the meat into manageable chunks, which he knows the dog will assimilate quite easily without choking on it. The meat used should be butcher's meat shin of beef being particularly beneficial, although not always at a price to suit all pockets. Many breeders complain at the cost of butcher's meat, which is certainly high and it seems sensible that if you cannot afford to keep a dog on such food, then it is better to try and adapt him to meals which will cost less and provide for him probably equally as well! There are so many prepared dog foods on the market today, most of them offered by highly reputable firms with up-to-date laboratories and factories so that one cannot lightly reject them when planning a dog's menu at an economic price. Some people think highly of ox cheek, offal, paunches and such things. These are good, but like liver give best results when fed once a week only. Dog biscuits are essential, there being many different kinds to choose from and you will soon get to know what your dog likes best and what suits him. Following any trial of biscuits and/or new type feeding, always keep an eye on the dog's main motion that day and the following two days. This will tell you if the stuff suits his stomach or not. Fish is excellent food for the dog, and the fishmonger has quite a large variety of cheap fish suited to him, but again fish feeding is for the menu no more than twice a week at the most. It should be used, like some of the canned goods more as a change of diet or to add zest to an ordinary dish, rather than as a staple diet. Always make sure with fish that every bone has been removed. It is better fed either boiled or steamed, from which the dog will gain most nutriment. Eggs and milk are, of course, essentials, especially milk and a dog ought to have avail-

'Sasha' from an old picture brought to England in the 1880s by Mr. Berg, a member of the British Embassy in Moscow.
Courtesy Mrs. P. Barham

able a bowl of fresh milk daily. Vegetables and potatoes are not suitable for dogs and if forced upon them usually causes digestive upsets. The dog himself knows this instinctively and confines himself as a rule to green grass which he eats, often as an emetic.

The adult Borzoi, considering his size is not a huge eater and can exist well on a single meal a day (say, $1\frac{1}{2}$ lb. meat) sufficient to feed many breeds of half his size. However, a certain standard of condition and muscle has to be maintained and to this end the breeder must always strive. Obviously, if your dog looks scrawny and thin it is reasonable to assume he is not getting enough meat and the amount must be increased accordingly. If a Borzoi appears hungry it is apparent that he can be fed more, for the breed is not a greedy one, unlike the Pug who will go on eating almost to bursting point! Always keep an eye on your dog when he is feeding. You will see how he tackles his meal; if a Borzoi goes through it fast and seems to seek more then it is probable that he wants more. If he gets two-thirds of the way through the meal then eats the rest as though he could not care, then he probably does not care and your put-down quantity is slightly in excess of enough.

All dog feeding and husbandry is largely a matter of commonsense and you should learn to know your dog so well that you will become aware of any variation, however slight, which arises in his manner and/or make-up. Additives, such as 'Vetzymes' in Phillips' Yeast Product, are extremely useful, creating a healthy appetite in the dog and aiding the dog's mental outlook quite noticeably. Most breeders keep a stock of these useful tablets and have found them extremely beneficial. Cod liver oil is useful in the winter months with olive oil best used when the weather is hot. Malt extract is recommended as a bodybuilder. It is not necessary to give more than one teaspoonful of these oils daily to any adult. Cod liver oil is conveniently available in veterinary form. Vitamins too can be obtained in capsules and in tablets and these can be used with advantage, although it is advisable to have the doses prescribed by your veterinary surgeon, or other professional adviser. 'Abidec' can be bought in liquid or capsule form and is good for administering vitamins A, B, C, D and E. 'Calsimil' and 'Collo-Cal-D' which contain a balanced form of calcium for dogs with phosphorus and vitamin D are two preparations particularly good for curbing excitability in a nursing dam or to replace calcium deficiency when this is noted.

In conclusion, never feed poultry and game unless just the carved flesh is given. The bones are very dangerous to a dog and whereas if your Borzoi should catch a rabbit and eat it the same day, he will come to no harm, if the carcass remains to be eaten next day the hardened bones will constitute a real danger to his innards.

Mrs. E. Ruggles' Phoenix of Matalona

Miss B. Murray's Ch. Moryak of Moskowa

Mrs. W. Chadwick's Winjones Dunyashka

Chapter 6
General Management

Training

No one enjoys having an ill-trained dog and it is clear at times that the dog himself does not enjoy being ill-trained! He does not want to be continually reprimanded and shouted at, which so many owners seem to do merely because they have not bothered to show their dog what to do and how to do it. A badly trained dog reflects on an owner's ability at training and becomes a possession which is not appreciated as a good dog should be. The real Borzoi has a strong and positive character and coupled with this he is a big, powerful dog. Firm handling is essential, therefore in order to maintain him comfortably in the family circle, and train him to do what *you* want rather than have him do what he wants.

Most people prefer a puppy to train. It is simpler as you are starting with virgin material, no one else having had a hand in shaping or mis-shaping the animal's behaviour. But be firm right from the beginning; too many owners laugh and enjoy a young puppy's early capers, its exuberance and clumsiness, only to realize too late that the dog has grown up and acquired some irritating ways as normal habits! It becomes then rather difficult to break him of these unwanted characteristics, certainly not without a good deal of pressure on the part of the trainer.

Borzois from the Springett Kennels

Photo: Anne Cumbers

Miss B. Murray's Ch. Moryak of Moskowa

In the Home

The first lesson a puppy must learn is house-cleanliness. Borzois make quite large puddles and the sooner a youngster is encouraged to perform his natural functions outside, the better. If in a flat, a sand-tray will have to be used; in a house, then he must learn to use the garden. The first word he must get to know the meaning of is 'No'. Thus, when he makes a puddle he should be picked up, taken to the puddle, and shown it quite closely. At the same time say 'No' quite forcefully so that he knows you are annoyed. Then either set him firmly on to the sand-tray, holding him there for a few moments or put him outside in the garden and close the door on him. He will soon catch on and his training can be helped if you remember that a small puppy sleeps a good deal and that when he wakes up he will invariably want to urinate. Keep an eye on him while asleep and the instant he wakes up, pick him up without waiting for him to amble around and set him at once either on to his sand-tray or outside in the garden. Keep him there watching until he has passed his motion. Try and do this every time and before long you will have him properly trained, going straight to the tray or the door as soon as he awakens. Remember though, that if by chance you are not there to open the door or see him on to his tray that he must not be blamed. Then it is your fault for not being around to help him. Make sure that you never scold him in or after such circumstances, and remember to praise him when he does correctly what he has been trained to do. At night, he is sure to forget himself and who can blame a small puppy making a puddle over a lonely six-or eight-hour period? If you keep him in the kitchen at night, cover the floor with old newspapers, so that in the morning you can gather these up quickly and dispose of them with the mess he will have made. Never leave an untrained puppy in a room where he can create damage. People will tell you at times that their new puppy has torn up furniture, cushions, slippers and such things. It is not the puppy's fault—it is theirs, for leaving a raw youngster in a place where it could do such damage. Make sure that small puppies are either left in completely bare rooms or boxed when you go out or retire for the night. Never chastise a puppy or he will lose faith and confidence in you and the retention of these loyalties is very important if you are to be his successful trainer. Some trainers like to have around a rolled-up newspaper to emphasize the word 'No' in their training. This implement makes a lot of noise but it does not hurt. Often it is effective in synchronizing its use with the word of command. Later, as the puppy becomes better educated it can be dispensed with—the word 'No' alone will be found sufficient for getting good results.

On the Leash

The young Borzoi will need to learn all about the outside world as soon as possible. Up to the age of four months by which time he will have all his protective inoculations, he can be trained on the leash within the confines of your garden or home. Put on a leash he can be led up and down the garden, kept always on the left-hand side of the handler so that he learns a straight and steady action without pulling or dragging back. Keep such training to no more than ten minutes at a time so that he does not get bored or stale at the work. You can keep the rolled-up newspaper by you during this period. If the pupil pulls forward on the leash, thereby throwing out his shoulders, he should be tapped on the muzzle with the newspaper and given the command 'Back' or 'Heel'. He will soon learn that he must not pull forward. If he draws behind, dragging his rear along the ground he must be encouraged to come forward with either words of reassurance or by bribing him with a titbit, together with a firm pull on the leash which will activate him into forward action.

Once the pupil has shown promise he can be taken into the outside world. At first, he may be bemused at the noise and bustle, but this will soon pass off and he will move forward with confidence. Later, when he arrives at a time for show training, you will have the elementary lessons already instilled into him.

Mrs. E. Etheridge's Rodgivad Buccaneer at 11 months

With Children

Borzois are very protective and highly sensitive. They seem to like children and make good members of a family circle where children live and play. As with all breeds it is best to have the children first and the dog afterwards, introducing the dog as a small puppy so that he enters the family and grows up in it, when it will be found that he takes over almost as a nursemaid, the younger members of the home.

Exercise

The breed is one which can take a good deal of exercise, but this must not be overdone. If you keep a number of dogs and puppies, it is wise to allow a generous run outside every kennel. The dogs can exercise at will and the puppies will play, usually until they are ready to sleep. The wise owner never leaves around in the kennel any item, toy or food which could be quarrelled over. Regular walking exercise on the lead is a good thing for the Borzoi. Let him loose in the wide open spaces but make sure that no one has running free near by their small pet dog. Borzois are coursing hounds and it is their nature to chase any living moving object. The average Borzoi can keep up for miles with a horseman out for a canter and can easily cover many miles on foot being quite able to out-distance his owner. Mrs. Winifred Chadwick in her *The Borzoi Handbook*, 1952, writes that she exercises her 'Winjones' Borzois (which are very famous) beside a bicycle, but recommends quiet country roads for this practice. She says the dogs cover ten miles or so at a brisk trot without the least slackening of enthusiasm. She comments how good such exercise is for the dogs' feet. It sounds the ideal way of exercising Borzois.

Care should be taken in the exercising of young puppies. It can ruin a youngster to overdo the daily routine and even with a dog such as the Borzoi, the time given to exercising him should be *gradually* increased as the dog grows on. It is best to train your dog to walk the distance you take him on a slack lead, and cinder and rough paths are better for his feet than grass. Regularity is the key-note of success in exercising, which is a dog's second important need after his food. If the weather is inclement never let him down by staying indoors and depriving him of his outing.

Mrs. E. Etheridge's Rodgivad Brigand

Grooming

To look at a Borzoi you would think his coat presented an owner with many problems in the way of care and attention. Oddly enough, this is not so and the breed seems to have a coat which is unique, being very shiny and not inclined to carry dirt or dust. Of course, the coat should receive daily attention both in the form of brushing and combing, but it is not necessary to wash the coat so regularly as some breeds seem to require. This is indeed fortunate for bathing a Borzoi is quite a task and can seldom be effected by one person. If it has to be done, start at the tail end first washing part of the coat and body at a time while working towards the head. A thorough drying down with warm towels in an even temperature should then follow and when the dog is dry take him out for a brisk canter to get the blood circulating

Mrs. M. Ellison's Chanctonbury Delight with friend

well. No trimming is needed with this breed but plenty of attention with the brush and comb will usually pay handsome dividends. The ideal brush is the one with well-spaced bristles set in a rubber pad base. These are available at any pet store. At grooming time check the dog's eyes, ears, teeth, gums and under and round the tail, making sure that these areas are healthy and clean. The breed's moulting tendencies are well-known, dogs shedding their coats rather less than do bitches but plenty of other breeds are inclined to more profuse moulting and it lasts for only a short time.

Guarding

The Borzoi cannot be claimed a naturally aggressive guard, which is probably a good thing in view of its great size and power. However, an owner will find that his Borzoi will have a strong deterring effect on would-be intruders. Once upset, the breed can prove very formidable and being quite possessive of territory one can easily be trained to guard both home and owner. Note however, the breed is not a vociferous one.

Kennel or Indoors?

When a Borzoi is kept as a pet there seems no point in providing a kennel for him. He should be part of the family circle and live indoors with his own bed and trained to conform to the usual rules and regulations of the home. Most abodes can find a space for a pet even one as large as a Borzoi. If they cannot, then in fairness to the dog they should never have bought one! There are some strong and useful canvas based beds for dogs on the market, although it is not always easy to procure the really large ones such as you will require. A Borzoi bed should be at least 36 inches by 30 inches, rather bigger if you can manage it. It should be raised about 5–6 inches off the floor level for comfort and to avoid under-door draughts.

Given such accommodation for his sleeping hours the dog is well set up. He will learn quickly what is wanted of him and know when to be 'seen and not heard' as required. His intelligence and mental reflexes will be developed better than were he kept alone in an outdoor kennel and not only will he enjoy life better but give you, as his owner, much pleasure too.

Of course, if you keep a number of Borzois you must kennel them. There are a number of good pre-fabricated kennels available on the market today. In fact, there are models to suit every breed and most pockets. If you buy one, or perhaps make one from your own specification, make sure it is large enough for the dogs to move around comfortably. Every kennel should have its own run and this should be strongly constructed and high, for Borzois are great jumpers. The run system has a great advantage in that the dog can get plenty of fresh air, can play freely with others and attend to his functions out there instead of inside the kennel. Make the kennel high enough for yourself and visitors to stand inside without crouching. This means that you should allow at least six feet from floor to ceiling if this is practicable. Assuming that you intend to start a kennel which is to become established as a breeding and exhibiting venture you will need four connecting kennels, with a single one placed well away from them to be used as a 'hospital' bed if needed. Try and arrange for a small cupboard to be built on to the end of the range of four in which you can keep all the paraphernalia of the kennel—brooms, brushes, pails, shovels, wood wool, sawdust and disinfectant. Four kennels will keep any novice busy for a time, then when he is ready to graduate into more ambitious dimensions he can add to the range, provided space permits.

Try and arrange for the kennels to be built on well-drained gravel or sandy soil, preferably facing south or south-west. If you can, erect it not under trees, but with near-by trees protecting it from the prevailing winds of the district, so much the better. The whole structure should be raised well off the ground level and the kennel floors should be of wood. If any refinements are to be introduced then include slide-out sleeping benches as these can be removed and scrubbed at will. Whereas, with the Borzoi you do not have to worry about heating in the winter months—he does not seem to need it, but ventilation and complete freedom from draught is essential. The runs themselves should be laid of well pressed down cinder or screened breeze to the extent of at least six inches. This will allow for good drainage and it is better than concrete not only for this reason, but because it keeps the dogs' feet firm and well-knit. The best form of bedding is wood-wool, and although the dogs seem to like straw better the latter is inclined to harbour vermin and one cannot always guarantee its perfect cleanliness.

In conclusion, try and install the kennel with electric light, making sure that all cables and connections enter the kennel at points where they are inaccessible to the dogs, Borzois being inveterate chewers. Scrupulous hygiene must be observed at all times, going into every nook and cranny with disinfectant and scrubbing down the exterior with a strong antiseptic germicide.

Miss B. Murray's Ch. Zest of Fortrouge

Chapter 7
Exhibiting

Dog exhibiting is today a popular pastime in most lands where the pedigree dog has established himself. It is an interesting hobby and one which many Borzoi owners have embraced in recent years. However, the breed's numbers are perhaps too few as yet for it to make sufficient impact on championship shows at a nation-wide level. Breeds such as the Cocker Spaniel, the Cairn and Fox Terrier, whose numbers are legion compete for the challenge certificates offered to them at virtually every big championship event. Not so the good Borzoi who, because his breed's registration figures at the Kennel Club are comparatively small, must rest content for the moment with only a small number of shows where he can strive for a much-coveted challenge certificate to put him on the path for his title of champion.

However, a champion's title is the aim of the ambitious and experienced exhibitor. The newcomer to the show ring has to rest content with more modest activities, and a number of different types of show are available from which he can choose. Generally, they are breed shows where he will compete against other Borzois and any-variety events where the classes are usually of different breeds competing on their respective merits, one against the other. The former sort are, of course, the more popular as every Borzoi owner likes to know how his dog compares with another Borzoi and this is what the judge is there to do—put the Borzois one, two, three and so on in order of merit, *according to his opinion*. It is his opinion that counts on that day, at least. The following week, another judge with the same dogs before him, may well reverse or assort the first man's placings, because he will be judging to *his* opinion. This is why dog shows continue; if every judge did the same thing, i.e. put the same dog first, the same second and so on, everyone would become bored and give up the game. It is the atmosphere of chance coupled with competition which makes dog showing so interesting and brings more and more devotees to its ranks. The other type of show where you exhibit your Borzoi's good points against those of another breed's or breed's prime features, is rather different. The judge is supposed to know all about all the breeds he has before him, and then after judging them pick out the best three or four for prizes. That sometimes the element of chance involved in this procedure is high, goes without saying, and exhibiting at such shows, especially when the classes are well-filled is more of a 'game'. However, they do offer a form of training in show procedure for novice dogs and novice owners and in the absence of Borzoi specialist shows they should be patronized. Often enough, the fine upstanding and elegant Borzoi by his very presence and beauty will 'stand out' in the show ring and be chosen the winner!

It is at this point that a newcomer to the show ring has to be on his guard. It is easy, following such an unexpected win (one 'out of the bag' so to speak) to become tremendously enthusiastic, cast all caution to the wind and go out and buy three or four new Borzois to start a breeding kennel! This might seem an exaggeration, but older breeders will know it has happened and it goes on happening in every breed. The trouble is that so often the dog-show game, at first an exhilarating pastime can become almost at once a business imbued with rivalry and jealousy when such things occur. No novice should wax too keen with his dog until it has become established he has a good and promising exhibit. He should maintain a stable attitude to his dogs and the exhibition world, avoiding the *coteries* and *cliques* which abound in most competitive circles and undoubtedly exist in dogdom. By doing so, he will enjoy Borzois and the company of his friends in the breed, one which is noted for its cameraderie and comparative freedom from the ring-side gossip which seems to beset many worthy breeds.

Mr. and Mrs. R. Searle's Ch. Francehill Joker

The Different Types of Show in Britain

Exemption

THIS is a very small event, held usually in conjunction with a holiday-time fête and judged by some notability who may or may not know much about dogs. You can enter at this type of show without your dog being registered at the Kennel Club but this body's disciplinary rules have nevertheless to be observed. Only four classes for pedigree dogs may be scheduled where the breeds must be judged according to their breed Standards, but the classes fall into the Any Variety category and no specialist breed classes will be found. The remaining classes are for want of a better word termed 'novelty' classes and in these mongrels and cross-breds can compete. Such classes as 'Dog in Best Condition', 'Dog with the Most Soulful Eyes' and similar prove very popular with the public, but any win at such a show must be taken in very light vein.

Mr. Reg Bassett's Ch. Alexi of Colhugh and
Ch. Tina of Colhugh   *Photo: Pearce*

Sanction

The Sanction show has for a long time been regarded as an ideal training ground for up-and-coming exhibitors. This type of show is also used extensively by noted breeding kennels to bring out youngsters and yearlings with championship promise. Consequently, the true novice with a Borzoi he wants to try out, can quite easily find himself 'swamped' with the *crème-de-la-crème* around him. It is advisable to enter in perhaps three classes when attending such a show. The Puppy and Maiden classes are usually well-filled with mixed breeds but a striking variety such as the Borzoi stands a reasonably good chance of getting into the first three awards, provided he is a good specimen, of course. Perhaps he has even a better chance than he would in a breed class at the same show with only six or seven entrants. These are matters which need assessing and the recruit to the exhibition world will soon learn by experience in which classes he stands the most chance of winning. The Limited show, so called because entry is limited to a certain number of classes can be assessed in a similar manner. Both types of show are restricted or confined to the members of the club or society promoting the event and challenge certificate winners are not eligible.

Open

This type of show can be benched or otherwise as the promoters and/or the Kennel Club see fit. Often they are held in conjunction with an Agricultural Show or County Show and are frequently open-air events. Conditions are similar to those enforced at a championship show, but no challenge certificates are available at open shows. At the open air all-breed events, competition in the breeds is often sparse, and many exhibits of less than average worth can come away with important prize awards. However, if the open show is one organized specifically by a breed society such as the Borzoi Club then the best in the breed will be on show and the competition will probably be fierce.

Championship

Championship shows are benched events. They are the most important shows and always well attended as challenge certificates are on offer (as a rule) and these are avidly sought after by exhibitors. Sometimes these shows will run for two, even three days, although the hound group into which Borzois fall will be judged on only one of these days. Cruft's Dog Show schedules almost every variety, offering challenge certificates to most. Some experienced exhibitors aver that it is just as easy to win at a championship show as it is to take an award at a mere Sanction show. Most judges will agree that this often is true and will be able to recall instances when they have been confronted with dogs at championship shows which have gone into the prize awards and which previously they have been unable to place at a Sanction show!

The question is—what sort of show to attend when you are a novice? Personally, I favour breed classes to any other sort, but the Borzois are usually ill-catered for because most show managements only put on breeds which are likely to bring them in a profit, or at least strike even, financially. The Borzoi Club is fully aware of this situation and guarantees classes at important events in an effort not only to publicize the breed but to encourage owners and breeders to exhibit. Every Borzoi owner ought to join this go-ahead club and support shows where the Borzoi is scheduled. If you love the breed you will want to see it thrive and develop. The Limited shows are perhaps preferable to sanction shows because the latter permits the entry of mature

Borzois, some of whom may well have done a good deal of winning and represent insurmountable competition to the youngster being tried out. Open shows too, offer the novice exhibitor a sound opportunity, for again he will find Puppy, Maiden and Novice classes to try his hand against dogs who are probably no better, no worse than he. There is a trend in many societies to put on Beginners' and Special Beginners' classes in the various breeds and this is a move to be applauded for many new Borzoi owners need encouragement in the general world of dogs.

The Match

This is conducted under Kennel Club Rules and Regulations, being a competition on the 'knock-out' system between pairs of dogs, whether of the same breed or invited breeds. The main purpose of the Match is to give interest and education to club members. A small prize is usually awarded to the winner.

In conclusion, if you plan to make a hobby of dog showing, read the rules. This means not only the rules of the club or society where you plan to exhibit, but the Kennel Club Rules and Regulations too. These are quite rigid and will be strictly enforced for dog exhibition has been brought to a high level procedure by the Kennel Club who since it was founded in 1873 has eliminated the many malpractices of early days and now controls the breeding and exhibition of dogs.

Preparing for the Show

To make any real impact at your first show you must at least try and present your dog in a way that his good points will be effectively displayed and he will parade with a fine degree of deportment. This means that not only must the dog himself be trained to show, but you may need to give yourself a modicum of training too. A dog and his handler are in effect very little different from a theatrical 'double act'. Both play an important part in the effort to achieve success—in this case it is a first prize, and later, who knows, a challenge certificate. Consequently, both dog and handler need to be on their toes as it does not rest entirely with the dog and his points, but the way they are presented.

The Borzoi being a big dog is not particularly easy to manœuvre or place. However, it is possible that having had him from a puppy and having commenced his training when he was four or five months old that there will be an understanding between you and he will readily interpret the merest twist of your wrist on his leash and respond at once. If this ideal state does not exist then you must start at once to train your exhibit towards this end. For instance, he must be taught to enter the ring elegantly and with confidence so that the judge may assess the value of his general appearance. No judge appreciates a lunging or hang-back exhibit and any Borzoi entering the ring in either way will almost certainly lose points before he starts. The dog must be taught to stand firm at command, preferably in profile to the judge so that the beauty of his outline can be appreciated. However, if an exhibit is inclined to reveal certain faults in his make-up by posing this way, then the handler must learn to employ certain subtleties in his method of presentation to obscure or disguise them. To do this is perfectly legitimate and is an art in itself.

In effect, you must learn to handle your dog and show him to the judge by displaying his *best* points. If he has some bad points (and few dogs have not) keep them from the judge's eye as much as you can. If he is a clever judge he will find them quickly enough, but then only a certain percentage are 'clever' judges.

Most shows are unbenched, so it behoves you with a big dog to find yourself a cosy place somewhere in the hall where you will remain undisturbed until you are ready to exhibit. Corners are best where you can keep your Borzoi under control and stop inquisitive dogs from poking in their noses too closely. Lay down a cheap blanket and install yourself and dog until the first class in which you are entered becomes due.

The First Class

Soon you will hear your ring number called. You will know the number you hold because it will appear in the show catalogue against your dog's name. You will be told where to place yourself and your exhibit by the ring stewards. There are usually two of these, helping and supporting the judge. Their job is to usher in the exhibits as the various classes become due and in effect keep an eye on the orderly running of the ring. Once all the class exhibits are present and standing ready, the judge will commence judging. He will probably beckon you over to him and ask you to stand your dog in front of him. This you will do and he will run his hands over the dog and commence to assess his virtues and quality. All this time you will be taking care that the dog stands firm and square and behaves himself. The judge will want to look in his mouth and examine his teeth, gums and jaw formation. He may wish to do this himself or may require you to open your dog's mouth for him. Once he has gone over the dog, he will want you to move away from him to the other end of the ring. This you do so that he can see what the dog looks like behind as he moves off. He will see the hindquarters, the musculature and general action of the dog moving away. He

will get some idea as to the dog's soundness and type. Then when you get to the perimeter of the ring you will turn round and retrace your steps to where the judge is standing. As you return he will assess the dog's forward action, his front, poise and balance. He may even move over to the side of the ring and see how the dog performs as he passes by him. This is why when you train a Borzoi to show you should ensure he moves with style, even a little flamboyance. A big canine 'show-off' in the ring gets away with a lot. By his manner he can cover up a lot of deficiencies in his type and make-up. As has been said, a dog (and his owner) should be trained to be good actors, the dog show world being rather like the theatre. A dog can carry on a long time just 'looking' good, but eventually a perceptive judge is going to find out if he really *is* good. This is why the dogs who *look* good and are *really* good become the big winners. Those who do not merit full marks in both departments seldom make the grade. Poor ones fall heavily by the wayside in the course of their careers, no matter how well campaigned and advertised they have been. This is because Borzois are established in perhaps a closer circle than many other breeds and although competition in Borzois is not weighty numerically it is quite fierce in respect of its quality and individuals are closely judged and discussed intimately. Consequently any weaknesses in a dog's make-up are quicker sought out and revealed sooner than in a breed better populated.

Once the judge has decided which dog he prefers for first prize (red card) he will probably place it out in the centre of the ring facing the main body of spectators. Then other dogs will be selected to fill second (blue card), third (yellow card) and reserve (green card) places. Assuming that the judge is satisfied with his placings the steward will then receive his instructions to distribute the award cards. Always be on your guard right up to the last moment of judging to keep your dog on his toes, displaying himself to his best advantage. It is not unusual for a judge to change his mind just before the prizes are given and alter his placings. It can be a disappointment not to win, but to have a prize cancelled or curtailed right at the moment of triumph can prove quite desolating, especially if it was due to one's personal failure in ringcraft tactics.

Future Showing

Assuming that you have become an enthusiast and intend to continue exhibiting you will in due course be considering the competition of big championship shows. If your dog is just an average specimen you are unlikely to get to the top with him— a champion's title is for the super dog and no judge should ever award a dog a challenge certificate unless he is convinced that

Mrs. E. Etheridge's Rodgivad Moonraker (*left*)

the exhibit is one worthy of that title. Possibly, there are cases where dogs of rather less than top quality worth have achieved their titles mainly due to clever campaigning on the part of their owners. Fortunately, such cases are rare—they do no good, even harm, to the breed and the dogs involved are seldom accepted and/or bred to in normal circumstances. The really good dog usually makes the grade however, provided his owner does not give up or become disillusioned half-way along the dog's career. Exhibiting needs enthusiasm and dedication and determination in no small measure, especially if a champion's title is the aim. You need three challenge certificates awarded by three different judges, with one of the challenge certificates an award after the dog has become twelve months of age.

Championship shows are benched events. The benches are galvanized three-sided pens for accommodating the dogs while they are not actually in the show ring being exhibited. Every dog has its catalogue number affixed above its head on the bench, and this allows visitors to the show to inspect the exhibits at will. You will require a bench chain and it is a good idea to have a blanket or rug for the dog to rest upon. One end of the bench chain is affixed to the dog's collar and the other end is passed through a ring set into the rear of the bench and then clipped to the chain itself, according to the freedom you wish to allow your dog on his bench. It is wise to permit him just enough room to make himself comfortable, curl up and get to sleep. If you can, take a quick check on his neighbouring competitors. If they seem placid, so well and good, but if one appears nervous adjust the chain so that your dog's nose does not project beyond the extremities of the dividing panel. It is better to be safe than sorry.

As this type of show is usually a full-day affair and you are confined there win or lose, you should come well prepared. This means food and drink for the dog (the food not to be given him until *after* he has been judged); similar supplies for yourself, and enough suitable vessels to administer it. It is a good idea to have a pocket first-aid kit, but never forget the tit bits, so important to the average exhibit also the grooming tools. Given all these things you should be well set for the day ahead. It is to be hoped that you will do your share of winning and collect a few prize cards. If you manage to win your first or second challenge certificate you will be happy indeed, but remember—it is the third and final one to make your dog a champion which is the hardest and most worrying to get—at least, so they say!

Registrations

To maintain strength in the breed every Borzoi owner should register his puppies at the Kennel Club. Not only this, but he should make a point of encouraging other breeders to do the same. By so doing and keeping up a good total of figures every year, the breed can expect more acknowledgement from show organizers and this will mean more frequent classification for Borzois at leading shows. Apart from this there is always the chance of getting an increase in the number of challenge certificates on offer from the Kennel Club.

The annual figures of Borzoi registrations in England for the last quarter of a century are as follows:

1948	157	1960	119
1949	157	1961	119
1950	177	1962	183
1951	160	1963	121
1952	102	1964	203
1953	104	1965	137
1954	100	1966	208
1955	70	1967	273
1956	123	1968	320
1957	90	1969	271
1958	81	1970	293
1959	99	1971	206
		1972	393

These figures are taken from January to December in each year.

Glossary of terms

A

AFFIX. Term applied to a kennel name which is attached to either end of a dog's name in order to identify him with that kennel. The Kennel Club demand that actual *breeders* of the dog or its parents should put the Affix *before* the dog's registered name, while *non-breeders* of the dog should put the Affix *after* the dog's registered name. The Kennel Club has waived this rule until 1st January, 1976, for Affix-holders who compounded their kennel name before 1st January, 1971, and applied to the Kennel Club Committee for permission to be free from the positional limitations.

ANGULATION. The angles formed at the point where the bones meet at the joints. In the hind limb it refers to the correct angle formed by the true line of the haunch bone, the femur and the tibia. In the case of the fore legs it refers to the line of the shoulder bone, radius bone and humerus. A dog which lacks angulation possesses straightness in these joints and a condition such as this could be reasonably considered unsound.

A.O.V. Any Other Variety. This term indicates that class entries are valid from any other variety than the breed provided for in a previous class.

APPLE HEADED. A rounded head such as is seen in the top of the skull of the Toy Spaniel. Undesirable in most breeds.

APRON. The frill or long hair on the throat and brisket on long-coated breeds.

A.V. Any Variety. This term is used to indicate that entries are valid from *any* variety, including those provided for in earlier classes. It applies to 'beauty' shows, stakes and field trials.

B

B. or b. The abbreviation used for bitch (female), described in show catalogues.

BAD-DOER. A dog who does badly however well fed and cared for. Sometimes such a dog has seldom done well from birth.

BAD SHOWER. A dog who for reasons of pique, nerves or boredom will not or cannot display himself properly and well in the show ring.

BALANCE. Co-ordination of the muscles providing graceful action coupled with the dog's overall conformation. The lateral dimensions of the specimen should fuse pleasingly with the horizontal and vertical dimensions.

BARRELLED. This refers to the shape of the rib-cage. It should be long, strong, well-rounded and with plenty of spring, allowing plenty of heart room.

BAT EARS. Large, pricked ears like the bat's and as seen in the French Bulldog. A fault in many breeds.

BAY. The voice or call of a hound on the trail.

B.B. The abbreviation for Best of Breed. A dog who has beaten all others in his breed.

BEARD. The profuse, bushy whiskers of certain breeds such as the Brussels Griffon.

BELTON. The blue and white and orange and white flecked colour seen in certain English Setters.

BITCHY. The term for an effeminate or over refined male dog.

BITE. Refers to the position of the upper and lower incisors when the dog's mouth is closed.

BLAZE. A white, usually bulbous, marking running up the centre of the face of some dogs. Sometimes the term is used to describe a white collar marking on the coat.

BLOOM. Glossiness or good sheen of coat, suggesting the owner is in good condition.

BLOCKY. Term used to describe the brachycephalic head such as the Boston Terrier's. Sometimes the term is used to describe a short, stocky, cobby body such as the Bulldog's.

BLUE. A blue-grey colour such as seen in a pigeon and encountered in a number of breeds such as the Whippet and Bedlington Terrier.

BONE. A well-boned dog is one having limbs which give the appearance and feel of strength and spring without coarseness.

BR. Abbreviation for Breeder, i.e. owner of the dog's dam at the time of whelping.

BRACE. Two dogs or two dogs exhibited together.

BRINDLE. A mixture of light and dark hairs giving a generally dark effect, usually being lighter streaks or bars on a grey, tawny, brown or black background.

BRISKET. The part of the body which is in front of the chest and between the forelegs.

BROKEN COLOUR. Where the main coat colour is broken up with white or other coloured hairs.

BROOD BITCH. A bitch kept for breeding purposes.

B.S. An abbreviation for Best in Show or Best in Sex. A dog who has beaten all others in the show or all others in his sex, respectively.

BRUSH. A tail which has long bushy hair such as is found in the various Spitz breeds.

BURR. The irregular formation inside the ear.

BUTTERFLY NOSE. When the nostrils are mottled, i.e. showing flesh colour amidst the black or brown pigment.

BUTTON EARS. Ears which drop over in front covering the inner cavity such as in the Fox Terrier, for example.

C

CAT FEET. Short, round and tightly made feet with compact thick pads, the toes well muscled-up and arched, like a cat's.

C.C. Challenge Certificate. A Kennel Club award signed by a judge for the best dog of his sex in his breed at a Championship Show.

CH. Abbreviation for Champion. The holder of 3 C.Cs awarded and signed by three different judges.

CHARACTER. A combination of the essential points of appearance and temperament as assessed for the whole, and distinctive to the particular breed or variety to which the dog belongs.

C.D. Companion Dog. A dog holding this degree has passed a test for obedience and reliability.

C.D.(x) Companion Dog (Excellent). A dog holding this degree has passed a severe test for obedience and reliability.

CHEEKY. Exceptional development of the cheek muscles and cheek tissue.

CHINA EYES. Synonymous with Wall Eyes, which are eyes parti-coloured white-and-blue, uncommon except in such as merle Sheepdogs and some Corgis.

CLODDY. A low and thick-set build.

CLOSE-COUPLED. Short and nicely knit in couplings.

COBBY. Compact and neat and muscular in formation, i.e. like a cob horse.

CORKY. Compact, alert and lively in body and mind, well spirited.

COUPLINGS. The part of the body between the fore and hind limb joints.

COW HOCKS. When the hocks are bent inwards, thus throwing the hind feet outwards. A fault in any breed.

CROUP. The area adjacent to the sacrum and immediately before the root of the tail.

CROSS-BREED. The progeny of parents of two different pedigree breeds.

CRYPTORCHID. A male dog whose testicles are abnormally retained in the abdominal cavity.

CULOTTE. The feathery tail on the back of the forelegs, a term used mainly in such breeds as the Pekingese, Pomeranian and Schipperke.

CUSHION. The fullness of the foreface given by the padding of the upper lips in the Mastiff and Bulldog.

D

D. or d. The abbreviation for the male dog as described in show catalogues, etc.

DAM. The female parent of puppies. The term is in general use but it has special reference to the bitch from the time she whelps the puppies to the time when she has finished weaning them.

DEWCLAWS. The rudimentary fifth digits and claws found on the insides of the legs below the hocks. These are better removed from the puppies a few days after birth.

DEWLAP. The loose pendulous skin under the throat in some breeds such as the Bloodhound.

DISH FACED. When a depression in the nasal bone makes the nose higher at the tip than at the stop.

DOME. Term applying to the rounded skull in some breeds, such as the Spaniel.

DIMPLES. The shallow depressions at each side of the breastbone.

DOWN FACED. The opposite to dish faced when the nose tip is well below the level of the stop due to a downward inclination of the nose.

DOWN IN PASTERNS. Showing an angle of the front feet forward and outward instead of the correct pastern which should be straight in line from the forearm to the ground.

DROP EARS. Pendant ears which lie close and flat to the side of the dog's cheek or face.

DUDLEY NOSE. Wholly flesh coloured nostrils, usually cherry or coffee coloured, quite distinct from the Butterfly Nose.

E

ELBOW, OUT AT. When the elbows are not close to the body and the points of elbow stick outwards, as unsoundness in most breeds.

EXPRESSION. A combination of the emplacement, size, colour and lustre of the eyes, giving the face the aspect desirable to the particular breed or variety.

F

FALL. The long hair or fringe overhanging the face of some breeds.

FALSE HEAT. A type of heat or season which affects many bitches today. Those affected give every sign of experiencing a normal heat, but the symptoms are liable to disappear suddenly and even when mated, a bitch will fail to conceive.

FEATHER. The long hair or fringe at the back of the legs of some breeds. Sometimes refers to the fringe of hair beneath the tail.

FELTED. The term given to a matted coat.

FIDDLE HEAD. A long wolf-like head.

FILLED UP. A term given to the face when the cheek muscles are well-developed and depressions under the eyes are filled in with muscle or tissue.

FLAG. The long fine hairs beneath the tail. Sometimes referring to the tail itself.

FLARE. Another term for blaze.

FLECKED. When a coat is slightly ticked or dotted with another colour.

FLEWS. The pendulous inner corners of the lips and upper jaw.

FRILL. Refers to the hair under the neck and on the chest.

FRONT. What can be seen of the dog from the front, especially chest, brisket, forelegs.

FURROW. The groove or indentation running from the stop to near occiput.

G

GAIT. The dog's walk or movement generally.

GAY TAIL. A tail which is carried high above level of the back and the horizontal.

GOOD DOER. A dog which does well at his food and thrives without any special treatment.

GOOSE RUMP. When the croup falls away too sharply and abruptly, the tail being set-on too low.

GRIZZLE. An iron-grey coat colour or a coat colour giving a grizzled grey effect.

GUN SHY. A dog who is gun shy is fearful of a gun or its report.

GUIDE DOG. A dog trained to guide blind people.

H

HANDLER. A person who handles dogs for exhibition at shows. Although applying to anyone who does this, it refers usually to a professional handler.

HARD MOUTHED. A hard-mouthed dog is one who damages the game he is retrieving. Applies to Gundogs.

HARE FOOT. A rather long and narrow foot with the digits well supported as in the hare.

HARLEQUIN. A piebald or patched white and black coat, referring especially to a type of Great Dane.

HAW. The inner part of the lower eyelid, being well developed hangs down, often showing red as in the Bloodhound.

H.C. Highly Commended. An award in dog shows which indicates an exhibit of high merit, but carries (as a rule) no monetary value. Sixth in position.

HEAT. A bitch is said to be 'on heat' when she is in season, i.e. during her oestral period.

HEIGHT. A dog's height is usually measured vertically from ground to the withers, i.e. to the top of the shoulders.

HOUND MARKED. When the coat colour body patches conform to the conventional pattern of hounds, i.e. a dark saddle, dark ears and head and often with a patch at or near the set-on of tail. The rest of the coat is white.

HOCKS. The joints in the hind legs between the pasterns and stifles, similar to the ankle in humans.

HUCKLE BONES. The top of the hip joints.

HUND, HÜNDIN, HÜNDCHEN (German). Dog, Bitch, Puppy.

I

IN-BREEDING. The mating of closely related dogs, usually arranged in order to try for perpetuation of certain desirable points, already existing in the mating pair.

INTERNATIONAL CHAMPION. Abbrev. Int. Ch. A dog who has been awarded the title of Champion in more than one country. Not an officially recognized term.

K

KEEL. The absolute base of the body. A term usually applied to Dachshunds.

KINK-TAIL. A tail with a bend or kink in it.

L

LAY-BACK. The dog's nose when it lies well back into the face as in the short-faced breeds such as the Bulldog.

LEASH. The leather thong by which a dog is held. An old term for three coursing hounds.

LEATHER. The skin of the ear-flap.

LEGGY. High on the leg, making the dog seem out of balance.

LEVEL MOUTH. When the jaws are placed so that the teeth meet about evenly, neither undershot nor clearly overshot.

LINE-BREEDING. The mating of dogs of near or similar strain, not too closely related.

LIPPY. When the dog's lips overhang or are abnormally developed.

LITTER. Family of puppies born to the bitch at the same time of whelping.

LOADING. Refers to shoulders which are too heavy.

LOINS. That part of the body which protects the lower viscera overlying the lumber vertebrae between last ribs and hind-quarters.

LONG-COUPLED. The reverse to close-coupled.

LUMBER. Too much flesh and weight, giving the dog an ungainly appearance and rather clumsy in movement.

M

MAIDEN. Generally refers to an un-mated bitch, but is a term used in show circles to indicate an exhibit not having won a first prize.

MASK. The dark markings on the muzzle, even the muzzle itself.

MATCH. An elementary form of competition matching one dog against another until all entrants except the winner have been eliminated.

MATING. When a bitch is served by a dog, i.e. mated, when the act of copulation takes place.

MATRON. A brood bitch, one used for breeding.

MERLE. Blue-grey colour, usually marbled with black or black flecks, often found in working dogs.

MONORCHID. A dog with only one testicle visible and descended into the scrotum.

MUZZLE. The projecting part of the head (face) combining mouth and nose.

N

N.A.F. Name applied for.

N.F.C. Not for competition. Used on his bench or a show catalogue against his entered name to indicate that he is on display rather than for competition.

NOVICE. Usually refers to an inexperienced exhibitor or breeder, but in show world parlance a dog or bitch not having won two first prizes.

O

OCCIPUT. That part of the skull at the top and back which is prominent in some breeds, especially the hound family.

OESTRUM. The bitch's menstrual term. Sometimes referred to as her 'heat' or 'season'.

ON HIS TOES. Infers that an exhibit is well poised, confident and showing himself well in exhibition.

OUT AT ELBOWS. When the points of elbows stick outwards when seen from the front. A fault in most breeds.

OUTCROSS. The mating of dogs which are totally unrelated, although of the same breed.

OUT AT SHOULDERS. When the shoulders protrude outwards in a loose manner giving the effect of a wide front. A fault in most breeds.

OVERSHOT. When the incisors of the upper jaw project out and beyond the incisors of the lower jaw with a noticeable space between the teeth rows.

P

P. Puppy.

PAD. The cushioned or padded sole of the foot.

PARTI-COLOUR. A coat of two or more colours in patches or chequered form.

PASTERN. The lowest part of the leg below the knee and below the hock, equivalent to the wrist in the human.

PEAK. The term applied to the occiput when this is prominent in certain hounds and setters.

PEDIGREE. A genealogical tree, giving the names of the dog's parents and ancestors beyond, usually to the third or fourth generation.

PIED or PIEBALD. Term given to a coat of two colours, black and white in roughly equal proportions but placed irregularly over the body.

PIG-JAW. A badly overshot jaw—like that of the pig.

PILE. The dense undercoat of a long-coated dog.

PLUME. The soft hair on the tail of a breed such as the Pekingese, i.e. long and feathery.

PREFIX. An obsolete term for Affix.

PRICKED EARS. Ears which stand erect.

Q

QUARTERINGS. The junctions of the limbs, especially the hind-quarters.

R

RACY. Slight in body build, being rather long cast.

RANGY. Rather long bodied, but with some substance yet giving an impression of having loose limbs.

RED. A general term for the various shades of fawn found in dog coat colours.

RESERVE. The fourth place in awards in a class, as a rule. It can refer however, to a runner-up in a class or in a show.

RIBBED-UP. A compactly made dog with well barrelled ribs.

RING TAIL. A curled tail which describes almost a circle.

ROACH BACK. A back which arches upwards along the spine, starting at the withers and with emphasis over the loins.

ROAN. A mixture of white with blue or red in roughly equal proportions and well placed.

ROSE EARS. Ears which fold over exposing the inner burr.

S

SIEGER (m), SIEGERIN (f), German. Champion.

SABLE. When the outer coat is shaded with black over a light coloured undercoat, as in the Collie.

SADDLE. A saddle marking of black or brown on the back.

SEASON. When a bitch is on heat or menstruating she is said to be in season.

SECOND MOUTH. A dog's permanent mouth or teeth, i.e. when he has lost his puppy or milk teeth.

SECOND THIGHS. The muscular development of the hind legs between the stifles and the hocks.

SELF-COLOUR. When a dog's coat is of one colour.

SEPTUM. The thin line which divides the nostrils.

SERVICE. When a bitch is mated by a stud dog she is said to have been served by him. The act of copulation is known therefore, as a service.

SET-ON. The point where the root of the tail is set on to the hindquarters.

SHELLY. Term given to a dog's body which is narrow and shallow.

SHOULDERS. Well laid back shoulders, i.e. those with an angle made by the positioning of scapula and humerus. Upright shoulders when the angle is obtuse will produce a mincing gait.

SIRE. The male parent of a dog, or bitch.

SOFT MOUTH. A dog with a soft mouth is able to retrieve game without causing it damage.

SPLAY FEET. Feet in which the digits are widespread.

SPRING. A term which refers to elasticity of rib, i.e. when the ribs are well-rounded and elastic.

STAND-OFF. The ruff or frill which stands-off from the neck of some Spitz breeds.

STANDARD. The official description of the breed, drawn up by a panel of experts and approved and published by the Kennel Club. It is used as a guide in judging and breeding.

SICKLE HOCKS. Hocks which are well bent and let down as in most breeds built for speed.

SNIPY. A muzzle which is too long and too weak and pointed.

STERN. Another name for tail, used mainly in hunting circles. Can refer to a dog's rear end.

STIFLE. The joint in the hind leg joining the first and second thighs and roughly equivalent to the knee in humans.

STOP. The depression or stop between and in front of the eyes.

STRAIGHT HOCKS. Hocks which are virtually straight, i.e. lacking resilience and bend.

STRAIGHT STIFLES. Stifles which lack bend and render a dog's gait untypical.

STRAIGHT SHOULDERS. Shoulders which are not laid back and lack angulation, causing a dog to move with stiff action.

STUD DOG. A male dog kept mainly for breeding purposes and for which a stud fee is charged to the owner of a visiting bitch.

SUFFIX. When the Affix (or kennel name) is joined on the end of a dog's registered name, e.g. 'Rimski of Rydens', 'Rydens' being the kennel name used in this instance as a Suffix.

SWAY BACK. A back which dips behind the shoulders because of poor muscle structure and development.

T

TRANSFER APPLIED FOR. Abbreviation T.A.F.

TEAM. Three or more dogs of any one breed.

THROATY. Showing an excess of loose skin about the throat.

TICKING. Small marks of another colour appearing on a darker or lighter main coat colour.

TIE. The term used to describe the locking union of dog or bitch during copulation.

TIMBER. Good bonal and body construction and quality.

TUCKED-UP. When the loins are well lifted as in racing and coursing dogs.

TULIP EARS. When the ears are carried erect, being slightly open and set at an angle which is slightly forward.

TRICOLOUR. Three different colours in the coat, referring particularly to black, white and tan.

TROUSERS. The hair on the hindquarters of a breed such as the Afghan hound.

TYPE. The quality and appearance essential to a dog if he is to epitomize the ideal model of his breed based on the description imparted by the particular breed Standard.

U

UNDERSHOT. When the lower incisors project beyond the upper incisors with a noticeable space between the rows of teeth, as in the Bulldog.

UNSOUND. A dog can be said to be unsound if he is unhealthy, unable to fulfil his work, is in very bad condition, and fails in movement and true character. A deformed or vicious dog may be permanently unsound whereas a dog recovering from an accident which affects his movement may well be temporarily unsound.

V

VENT. This generally refers to the anus or area around it.

V.H.C. Very highly commended. An award in the show ring which while giving fifth place carries no monetary prize.

W

WALL EYES. See China Eyes.

WEEDY. Puny and lightly constructed, lacking substance.

WELL-SPRUNG. Refers to a dog's ribs which should be well rounded and with plenty of spring.

WHEEL BACK. An arched or convex back.

WHELPS. Puppies which are newly born.

WITHERS. The point where the neck joins the body at the top of the shoulders region.

A Selected Bibliography

ONLY three* of the following books deal purely and simply with the Borzoi. The remainder are general books and/or fiction, containing material contributing to a serious study of the breed.

ASH, E. C.: *Dogs: Their History and Development*, London, 1927.

'ASHMONT': *Kennel Secrets*, Boston, 1893.

BARNETT, F. H.: *Our Dogs' Birthday Book*, London, 1902.

BARTON, F. T.: *Dogs*, London, *c*.1910.

BROWN, CAPT. T.: *Biographical Sketches and Authentic Anecdotes of Dogs*, Edinburgh, 1829.

BUFFON, M. LE COMTE: *Histoire Naturelle*, 1755, 1789.

*CHADWICK, MRS. W.: *The Borzoi Handbook*, London, 1952.

——*Borzois*, Halesworth, 1971.

COMPTON, H.: *The Twentieth-Century Dog*, London, 1904.

DALZIEL, H.: *British Dogs*, London, 1881.

DE BYLANDT, COMTE H.: *Les Races des Chiens*, Bruxelles, 1897.

DRURY, W. D.: *British Dogs*, London, 1901.

FARMAN, E.: *The Dog Owners' Annual*, London, 1904.

GRESHAM, F.: *Everybody's Book of the Dog*, London, *c*.1900.

*GUY, E. H.: *Mythe Borzois*, Taunton, n.d.

HARDING-COX: *Dogs: By Well-known Authorities*, London, 1906–8, which includes a folio *Newcastle—The Borzoi* of 11 pages, two full-page plates, one in colour, by the Duchess of Newcastle.

HUBBARD, C. L. B.: *Working Dogs of the World*, London, 1947.
Hutchinson's Dog Encyclopaedia, London, 1935.
JAQUET, E. W.: *The Kennel Club*, London, 1905.
JOHNS, R. and NAYLOR, L. E.: *Dogs for Profit*, London, 1937.
KNOWLES, G. W.: *The Book of Dogs*, London, *c.*1920.
LANE, H. C.: *Dogs Shows and Doggy People*, London, 1902.
——*All About Dogs*, London, 1890.
LEE, RAWDON B.: *A History and Description of the Modern Dogs of Great Britain and Ireland*, London, 1894, and later editions.
LEIGHTON, R.: *The New Book of the Dog*, London, 1907.
——*The Complete Book of the Dog*, London, 1922.
MARPLES, THEO.: *Prize Dogs*, Manchester, 1903.
MARTIN, W. C. L: *The History of the Dog*, London, 1845.
MAYHEW, SEWELL and COUSENS: *Dogs and Their Management*, London, 1939.
MEYRICK, J.: *House Dogs and Sporting Dogs*, London, 1861.
*PLIEVIER, H.: *With My Dogs in Russia*, London, 1961, (translated from the German *Meine Hunde Und Ich*, Frankfurt-am-Main, 1957).
SHAW, VERO K.: *The Encyclopaedia of the Kennel*, London, 1913.
——*The Illustrated Book of the Dog*, London, 1879–1881.
SMITH, A. CROXTON: *All About Dogs*, London, 1931.
——(Edit.) Lonsdale Library, *Hounds and Dogs*, Vol. XIII, London, 1932.
——*British Dogs at Work*, London, 1906.
——*Everyman's Book of the Dog*, London, 1909.
SMITH, LT.-COL. C. H.: *Dogs*, Edinburgh, 1840.
STABLES, DR. G.: *Dog Owners' Kennel Companion and Referee*, London, 1890.
——*Our Friend the Dog*, London, 1892.
WALSH, J. H. ('Stonehenge'): *The Dog, Its Varieties and Management in Health and Disease*, London, 1896.
——*The Dog in Health and Disease*, London, 1845.
WEBB, H. (Edit.): *Dogs: Their Points, Whims, Instincts and Peculiarities*, London, 1872.
YOUATT, W.: *The Dog*, London, 1845.

Dog Show Catalogues

Birmingham, 1886, 1887, 1888, 1889, 1890, 1894, 1895, 1896, 1897.
Crystal Palace, 1890.
Kennel Club, 1891, 1892.
Cruft's, 1892.

The Kennel Club (Great Britain)

List of Fees

The Kennel Club deals with all matters concerning dogdom from its offices at 1–4 Clarges Street, Piccadilly, London W1Y 8AB (Tel. 01 493 6651) and will answer promptly any inquiry regarding pedigree dogs. With effect from 1st January, 1973, a revision of fees takes effect and these are given below:

Registration by Breeder	£0·50
Registration by any person other than Breeder	£1·50
Registration (Breeder's Declaration not signed)	£2·00
Registration (Obedience Record)	£1·50
Registration (Name not changeable) Additional Fee	£0·50
Re-registration	£1·50
Transfer	£1·00
Loan or Use of Bitch	£1·00
Change of Name	£5·00
Pedigrees—	
Three Generations	£2·00
Five Generations	£5·00
Export	£2·50
List of Wins (Entered in Stud Book)	£0·50
Registration of Affix	£3·00
Affix Maintenance Fee	£1·00
(Holders of Affix may compound on the payment of an extra £7·00)	
Assumed Name	£2·00
Registration of Title	£5·00
Maintenance of Title	£3·00
Formation of a Branch by a Registered Society	£3·00
Maintenance of Title of a Branch of a Registered Society	£3·00
Registration of Title of a Dog Training Club	£5·00
Maintenance of Title of a Dog Training Club	£3·00

Details of other fees for holding of shows and/or working trials are obtainable from the Kennel Club on request.

Index

Line drawings by Peter Diment